*Salvation Blues*

POETRY BY RODNEY JONES

*The Story They Told Us of Light* (1980)

*The Unborn* (1985)

*Transparent Gestures* (1989)

*Apocalyptic Narrative and Other Poems* (1993)

*Things That Happen Once* (1996)

*Elegy for the Southern Drawl* (1999)

*Kingdom of the Instant* (2002)

*Salvation Blues: One Hundred Poems 1985-2005* (2006)

# Salvation Blues

ONE HUNDRED POEMS, 1985–2005

## Rodney Jones

Houghton Mifflin Company  *Boston  New York*  2006

For information about permission to reproduce selections
from this book, write to Permissions, Houghton Mifflin Company,
215 Park Avenue South, New York, New York 10003.

Visit our Web site: www.houghtonmifflinbooks.com.

*Library of Congress Cataloging-in-Publication Data*
Jones, Rodney, 1950–
Salvation blues : one hundred poems, 1985–2005 / Rodney Jones.
p.  cm.
ISBN-13: 978-0-618-62430-0
ISBN-10: 0-618-62430-9
I. Title.
PS3560.O5263S25 2006
811'.54—dc22   2005010550

Printed in the United States of America

Book design by Lisa Diercks
Typeset in Clifford Eighteen

MP  10  9  8  7  6  5  4  3  2  1

*for Gloria*

# CONTENTS

New Poems (2005)

FROM

*The Unborn* (1985)

# REMEMBERING FIRE

Almost as though the eggs run and leap back into their shells
And the shells seal behind them, and the willows call back their
    driftwood,
And the oceans move predictably into deltas, into the hidden
    oubliettes in the sides of mountains,

And all the emptied bottles are filled, and, flake by flake, the snow
    rises out of the coal piles,
And the mothers cry out terribly as the children enter their bodies,
And the freeway to Birmingham is peeled off the scar tissue of fields,

The way it occurs to me, the last thing first, never as in life,
The unexpected rush, but this time I stand on the cold hill and watch
Fire ripen from the seedbed of ashes, from the maze of tortured glass,

Molten nails and hinges, the flames lift each plank into place
And the walls resume their high standing, the many walls, and
    the rafters
Float upward, the ceiling and roof, smoke ribbons into the wet cushions,

And my father hurries back through the front door with the box
Of important papers, carrying as much as he can save,
All of his deeds and policies, the clock, the few pieces of silver;

He places me in the shape of my own body in the feather mattress
And I go down into the soft wings, the mute and impalpable country
Of sleep, holding all of this back, drifting toward the unborn.

# SWEEP

The two Garnett brothers who run the Shell station here,
who are working separately just now,
one hunched under the rear axle of Skippy Smith's Peterbilt tractor,
the other humming as he loosens the clamps
to replace my ruptured heater hoses,
have aged twenty years since I saw them last
and want only to talk of high school
and who has died from each class.
Seamless gray sky, horns from the four-lane,
the lot's oil slicks rainbowing and dimpling with rain.
I have been home for three days, listening to an obituary.
The names of relatives met once,
of men from the plant where he works,
click like distant locks on my father's lips.
I know that it is death that obsesses him
more than football or weather
and that cancer is far too prevalent
in this green valley of herbicides and chemical factories.
Now Mike, the younger brother,
lifts from my engine compartment
a cluster of ruined hoses,
twisted and curled together like a nest of blacksnakes,
and whistles as he forages in the rack
for more. Slowly, the way things work down here,
while I wait and the rain plinks on the rims of overturned tires,
he and my father trade the names of the dead:
Bill Farrell for Albert Dotson,
Myles Hammond, the quick tackle of our football team,
for Don Appleton, the slow, redheaded one.

4

By the time the rack is exhausted,
I'm thinking if I lived here all year I'd buy American,
I'd drive a truck, and I'm thinking
of football and my father's and Mike's words
staking out an absence I know I won't reclaim.
Because I don't get home much anymore,
I notice the smallest scintilla of change,
every burnt-out trailer and newly paved road,
and the larger, slower change
that is exponential,
that strangeness, like the unanticipated face
of my aunt, shrunken and perversely stylish
under the turban she wore after chemotherapy.
But mostly it's the wait, one wait after another,
and I'm dropping back deep in the secondary
under the chill and pipe smoke of a canceled October
while the sweep rolls toward me from the line of scrimmage,
and Myles Hammond, who will think too slowly
and turn his air force jet into the Arizona desert,
and Don Appleton, who will drive out on a country road
for a shotgun in his mouth, are cut down,
and I'm shifting on the balls of my feet,
bobbing and saving one nearly hopeless feint,
one last plunge for the blockers
and the ballcarrier who follows the sweep,
and it comes, and comes on.

## FOR THOSE WHO MISS
## THE IMPORTANT PARTS

The year Truman fired MacArthur
my uncle returned
from the hospital at Decatur,
his left hand torn
from the wrist, milled
into a ghostly bin
of Martha White Self-Rising Flour.
While Oscar Garrett ranted,
"We ought to get the bastards
before they get the bomb,"
and his wife, Mildred, went
to the kitchen for more custard,
the blue stump slipped out
of its flannel sleeve,
puffy and knuckled
like the head of a cottonmouth.
I didn't know pain had a phantom,
a thorn, like frostbite,
that ran long and clean
to the bone of emptiness.
I don't know yet whether
the coal stove or shame
flushed my father's face
with roses. While important
history went on elsewhere,
while the tough March wind
punched the window frames
and kicked at the glass bulb

in the heel of the thermometer,
my father and uncle were
almost as old as I am now.
Now I wish I were Li Po
with a Yangtze and plum blossom
to praise, with a poem
hard as jade to lay
on the threshold of annihilation.
If MacArthur had marched into China,
the map would still be yellow,
or I would not remember
so much my uncle's good hand
cold on my brow, and how my eyes
fell then, out of shyness,
running along the floorboards,
passing over his brown shoes,
over the knots
with their difficult wings.

# I FIND JOY IN THE CEMETERY TREES

I find joy in the cemetery trees.
Their roots are in our hearts.
In their leaves the soul
of another century is in ascension.
I hear the rustling of their branches
and watch the exhausted laborers
from the Burgreen Construction Company
sit down in the shade,
unwrapping their ham and salami
and popping open their thermoses.
Apparently, they too are enamored
of the hickory and willow
at the edge of our cemetery.
They are stretching twine, building a wall
as though this could be contained.
Probably they do not think
of our grandmothers who are pierced,
and probably they do not want
to hear about Thomas Hardy,
who, if I remember, has been dead
longer than they have been alive,
and who gave to the leaves of one yew
the names of his own dead. Anyway
the only spirits I can call in this place
are the stench of a possum
suppurating in secret weeds
and the flies, who are marvelous
because their appetite is our revulsion.
Let the laborers go on. Right now

I wish I could admire the trees simply
for their architecture. All winter
the dying have set their tables
and now they are almost as black
as the profound waters off Guam.
A few minutes ago, when they started
in a slight breeze off the lake,
the many and patient sails,
I could see in those motions
a little of the world that owns me—
and that I cannot understand—
rise in its indifferent passion.

# THOREAU

It is when I work on the old Volvo,
lying on my back among the sockets,
wrenches, nuts, and bolts,
with the asphalt grinding the skin
over my shoulderblades, and with the cold grease
dripping onto my eyeglasses,
that I think of Thoreau
on his morning walks around the pond,
dreaming of self-sufficiency.
I think of the odometer that shows
eight circuits of the planet.
I drop the transmission and loosen
the bolts around the bellhousing.
I take it in both hands, jerk,
and it pops like a sliced melon.
Carefully, so I won't damage
the diaphragm, I remove the clutch
and place it on a clean cloth
beside the jackstand. I look
at the illustrations in the manual
and I think of the lists that Thoreau made.
By the time I get to the flywheel,
grease is clotted in my hair,
my knuckles are raw and bleeding
against the crankcase, and I am thinking
of civil disobedience. I am looking

up into the dark heaven of machinery,
the constellations of flaking gaskets,
and I am thinking of Thoreau's dry cow,
of his cornstalks splintered by hail.

# THE FIRST BIRTH

I had not seen before how the body opens,
the petals of liver, each vein a delicate bush,
and where something clutches its way into the light
like a mummy tearing and fumbling from his shroud.
The heifer was too small, too young in the hips,
short-bodied with outriggers distending her sides,
and back in the house, in the blue *Giants of Science*
still open on my bed, Ptolemy was hurtling toward Einstein.
Marconi was inventing the wireless without me.
Leonardo was secretly etching the forbidden anatomy
of the Dark Ages. I was trying to remember
Galen, his pen drawing, his inscrutable genius,
not the milk in the refrigerator, sour with bitterweed.
It came, cream-capped and hay-flecked, in silver pails.
At nights we licked onions to sweeten the taste.
All my life I had been around cows named after friends
and fated for slaughterhouses. I wanted to bring
Mendel and Rutherford into that pasture,
and bulb-headed Hippocrates, who would know what to do.
The green branch nearby reeked of crawfish.
The heavy horseflies orbited. A compass, telescope,
and protractor darted behind my eyes. When the sac
broke, the water soaked one thigh. The heifer lowed.
Enrico Fermi, how much time it takes, the spotted legs,
the wet black head and white blaze. The shoulders
lodged. The heifer walked with the calf wedged
in her pelvis, the head swaying behind her like a cut blossom.
Did I ever go back to science, or eat a hamburger
without that paralysis, that hour of the stuck calf

and the unconscionable bawling that must have been a prayer?
Now that I know a little it helps, except for birth
or dying, those slow pains, like the rigorous observation
of Darwin. Anyway, I had to take the thing, any way
I could, as my hands kept slipping, wherever it was,
under the chin, by tendony, china-delicate knees,
my foot against the hindquarters of the muley heifer,
to bring into this world, black and enormous,
wobbling to his feet, the dumb bull, Copernicus.

# A HISTORY OF SPEECH

That night my sophomore date wanted kisses.
I talked instead of the torn ligaments
in my ankle, crutches and Ace bandages,
parading like any arthritic
the exotic paraphernalia of my suffering
and, that failing, went further, bobbing
in the thesaurus of pain: the iron lung,
the burn, torture with water and bamboo.
She twisted a frosted curl around one finger.
It was then she touched the skin along my neck.
It was then I noticed for the first time
the strange wing beating in my mouth
and kissed her in a kind of flight
that plummeted and searched for branches.

Ah, but Tahiti of a thousand Tahitis!
Among the suckling cars of the drive-in,
trays of pomegranates, lingerie of surf.
Days I hurled papers onto the porches of invalids.
June nights I only had to open my mouth,
out came a flock of multicolored birds,
birds of all denominations and nationalities,
birds of nostalgia, the golden birds of Yeats,
birds trained in the reconnaissance of exclusive buttons.
Before I knew it I was twenty-two.
I was whispering into the ear of Mary,
the mother of Jesus. I was dreaming

in two languages I did not understand.
I was sitting in the bar of the Cotton Lounge,

railing against George Wallace, when the fist
rang in my stomach and I looked up
to a truck driver shouting down at me,
"Talk too much!" Talk too much into greasy
footprint, linoleum stinking of beer,
the thigh of that woman rising to leave.
Talk too much and understand I'm not to blame
for this insignificance, this inflation
in the currency of language. Listen:
whenever I hurt, the words turned their heads;
whenever I loved too much, they croaked and hopped away.
At my luckiest, I'm only saying the grace
the hungry endure because they're polite.
Learning speech, Demosthenes put pebbles in his mouth,
but my voice is haunted by softer things.

# THE LAUNDROMAT AT THE BAY STATION

When the separation hit me with its tonnage, self-soiling, guilt,
I used to go there, having no other choice, void of the machinery
        of renewal,
carrying a pillowcase of spoiled shirts slung over one shoulder, bundling
in a mildewed towel my knot of blue jeans, underwear, and dirty
        sheets, my legacy, my impossible dowry.
I think I had never been so lonely, and the girl Shirley, acned,
leafing through a magazine of teenage stars, who gave change
in the Kwik-Mart next door when the change machines were broken,
        seemed either
contemptuous or flirtatious, hot-tempered, feigning an incredible wound.
I could hear the cycles kick on and off and, underneath, the
        continuous roar
of water surging up from the valves, and I remember, once I was inside,
how the dark outside would grow rigid, as though I had entered,
after all of Oklahoma, the green and narcotic light of a truckstop
        restroom—
the rubber dispensers on the wall, the mirrors that magnify the pores.
Most of the customers I don't remember, but I can't forget
the divorcées in tight black stretch pants, cautiously sorting their lace
        panties, talking too loud
and pulling their stringy, cotton-headed kids out of the garbage pails,
whole families, sallow and almost retarded, and improbable younger
        girls,
big blondes who seemed to leap out of the rain, their hair frosted and
        piled high on their heads,
their spike heels clicking on the linoleum tiles gummy with diet soda.

It hurts me, that separateness, and how I lived then, mostly in one
    room, my bed a delirium of books,
everything else on the floor—dishes, fishing tackle, wadded sheets of
    typing paper,
the bedsprings leaning against one wall wired to a black-and-white TV.
Through the wall I heard arguments, then thuds, something heavy,
    maybe chairs
being thrown, doors slamming, then the bass throbbing over the weeping.
That year filth was the ledger I kept, marking each shirt, each towel.
Now that I'm happy, I need illness or blows before the laundromat
    rises from the ashes
of my fever and confusion, and I can tell my wife how I looked at this
    one's thighs
or that one's enormous and floppy breasts as she knelt to take her sad
    underthings
from the dryer; how much I wanted their vulnerability, their poverty
    and hatred still to be there
once I was happier; and how much I wanted happiness then, even there,
smelling the faint and artificial odors of lemon blossoms, searching
    the wire baskets
for the mates to mismatched socks, the crude angels of
    embarrassment.


Almost a year and a half of my life has been blocked out, washed
    clean, the disease
of the self quarantined, checked there, and I don't want to think
about the laundry spinning in each washer, the dryers stationed like
    robots,
and the rejected people waiting, as though for a simple resurrection.
I don't want a new life spun clean of its dirt and chaos. The day my
    wife's mother,

my wife, and I came down the mountain from Santa Tecla to La
     Libertad,
I had been waiting for the river that runs through that place, even
     with the war there,
the way the women, some with their blouses off, were sitting on the rocks
with baskets of laundry to be knuckled and scrubbed, the children
splashing in and out of the shallow green pools left in the dry season,
and stretched beside them the shirts for labor and the shirts for
     dancing, the shirts for God
and the shirts for dying, all were whitening, were slowly drying
     around their stains,
and the laughter and the Spanish came up to me through the almond
     trees,
purely and without reason, rising on the small wind like birds.

# THE MOSQUITO

I see the mosquito kneeling on the soft underside of my arm,
 kneeling
Like a fruitpicker, kneeling like an old woman
With the proboscis of her prayer buried in the idea of God,
And I know we shall not speak with the aliens
And that peace will not happen in my life,
 not unless
It is in the burnt oil spreading across the surfaces of ponds,
 in the dark
Egg rafts clotting and the wiggletails expiring like batteries.
Bring a little alcohol and a little balm
For these poppies planted by the Queen of Neptune.
In her photographs she is bearded and spurred, embellished
 five hundred times,
Her modular legs crouching, her insufferable head unlocking
To lower the razor-edge of its tubes, and she is there
 in the afternoon
When the wind gives up the spirit of cleanliness
And there rises from the sound the brackish oyster and squid
 smell of creation.
I lie down in the sleeping bag sodden with rain.
Nights with her, I am loved for myself, for the succulent
Flange of my upper lip, the twin bellies of my eyelids.
She adores the easy, the soft. She picks the tenderest blossoms
 of insomnia.
Mornings while the jackhammer rips the pavement outside my
 window,
While the sanitation workers bang the cans against the big truck
 and shout to each other over the motor,

I watch her strut like an udder with my blood,
Imagining the luminous pick descending into Trotsky's skull
    and the eleven days
I waited for the cold chill, nightmare, and nightsweat of malaria;
Imagining the mating call in the vibrations of her wings,
And imagining, in the simple knot of her ganglia,
How she thrills to my life, how she sings for the harvest.

# FOR THE EATING OF SWINE

I have learned sloppiness from an old sow
wallowing her ennui in the stinking lot,
a slow vessel filled with a thousand candles,
her whiskers matted with creek mud,
her body helpless to sweat the dull spirit.
I have wrestled the hindquarters of a young boar
while my father clipped each testicle
with a sharpened barlow knife, returning him,
good fish, to his watery, changed life.
And I have learned pleasure from a gilt
as she lay on her back, offering her soft belly
like a dog, the loose bowel of her throat
opening to warble the consonants of her joy.
I have learned lassitude, pride, stubbornness,
and greed from my many neighbors, the pigs.
I have gone with low head and slanted blue eyes
through the filthy streets, wary of the blade,
my whole life, a toilet or kitchen,
the rotting rinds, the wreaths of flies.
For the chicken, the cow, forgetfulness. Mindlessness
blesses their meat. Only the pigs are holy,
the rings in their snouts, their fierce, motherly indignation,
and their need always to fill themselves.
I remember a photograph. A sheriff had demolished
a still, spilling a hundred gallons of moonshine.
Nine pigs passed out in the shade of a mulberry tree.
We know pigs will accommodate
demons, run into rivers, drowning of madness.
They will devour drunks who fall in their ways.

Like Christ, they will befriend their destroyers.
In the middle of winter I have cupped my hands
and held the large and pliable brain of a pig.
As the fires were heating the black kettles,
I have scrupulously placed my rifle between pigs' eyes
and with one clean shot loosened the slabs
of side-meat, the sausages that begin
with the last spasms of the trotters.
O dolphins of the barnyard, frolickers
in the gray and eternal muck, in all your parts
useful, because I have known you, this is the sage,
and salt, the sacrificial markers of pepper.
What pity should I feel, or gratitude, raising you
on my fork as all the dead shall be risen?

# TWO GIRLS AT THE HARTSELLE, ALABAMA, MUNICIPAL SWIMMING POOL

Too much of the country in their walk—
as though each struggled
against a tree at the center of her body,
or their bare feet were shoes

that didn't fit, poverty in every step,
in every move, deliberate
as footsteps in plowed fields,
through clots of local boys, up

slippery rungs to the high board,
their bodies oiled, flipping away
casually the menthol cigarettes,
tossing back their bleached hair,

both twelve or thirteen years old:
like old houses, like mothers
pitched forward into the wind,
entering the cold, strange waters.

# DECADENCE

### 1

In the junque store the idlers were talking about primitives,
how scarred wood can be steeped in dignity, how that subtle
     patina
derives from hands, hands of the old, hands of the poor.
                              The hands of the dealer
were on the halltree, the cream separator, the set of burled,
chestnut tools, as he whispered, *Williamsburg, Jamestown,*
     *Monticello.*
He was selling an incarnation of this country, not mere
     furniture,
patched and splaying relics, like that pie safe, still hopeful
                           in its ugliness,
hewn crudely with a broadax, planed with bad iron for
     temporary uses.
I could remember how, in my grandmother's attic, dirt daubers
would construct their nests along the pegs
of an unworkable loom, and how one residential cell at a time
                           would crumble,
dusting the human heirlooms stacked in boxes underneath:
delicate Japanese fans, mother-of-pearl combs, letters
from flung hamlets named for springs, groves, and crossroads.
Under the spectacles that I had found in a stray boot
                           a bleached calligraphy
yielded its covered-dish suppers, its gaggle of Sunday
     visitations,

while time's odor, dull and implacable,
        stirred from a sidesaddle hooked on a rafter—
redolence of an old horse as he is being led from his last
        pasture.
Later, when the house was sold, the decadence broke out:
moths flopped sleepily from giant black trunks,
and spiders, those shrewd solicitors of corners, invaded
with light that leaked through shingle cracks,
gnawing the tablecloths, flawing the spokes of spinning wheels.
                                In the junque store
I could imagine the rage and falling away, the ordeal
of finishing and refinishing, the worship of smooth surfaces,
and the patient preservation of flaws. I could love things
for hands that touched them, before grace, setting the plain
        tables.


        2

In America there are many sacred places: improbable shrines,
                        Jerusalems of bed sheets,
dim synagogues where the spirit loiters, or sleeps, obsolescent
                        as that brakeman
I saw long ago on the L & N, waving his handkerchief from a
        caboose.
And here on my front porch, midnight, in Jefferson's paved
        Virginia,
all the good students are smoking dope and talking about God.
I watch them hesitate and plunge into history. They pass
the joint and I hear, in each voice, the blurred, icy dithyrambs
                        of Morpheus.

In each face I watch the moon that rises out of childhood,
                              largest light
against these small heavens resonating through
                              the wishful dark.
Here are our cosmic rose, our jockey of telepathy, our shaman
                              of the dime-store mantra.
The joint shrinks, passing from one to another, O orbital
         communion.


*When the spirit moves you, don't be ascared, spake!*
         Summer revival, 1958, Church of God,
I was watching, Mrs. Morgan
         was coming up like something partially
                              digested,
Mrs. Morgan was home from the nuthouse and she was
         coming
out of her pew like hot shrapnel of bad corn blasting the
         throat:
                              *O Savior . . . hare me, Lord!*
I have in me the creak of the wheelchair
         after the unsuccessful
                              laying on of hands,
the horror and beauty of it. I have belief rotting and going
bad in the stomach, old egg taste that comes to me like
         postcards
from places I'd rather forget. On the porch at midnight
                              the students
will grow silent. They will listen for the wind, the sweet
         summer evening,
a few stars diminishing slowly, darkening like the notes of a
         lullaby.

3

Once everyone was a Hemingway at the party where the girl
who painted penises stepped out of her clothes. Her pathetic
                              gosling neck of a body
clovered with goose bumps, and Christ! the luminous bad taste
                              of her art. I mean
banana penises rising from baskets of assorted fruits,
                              wienerwurst penises curled
in Dutch ovens, senile penises slumped in waterlogged dories,
                              symbolic dorks and phalluses
of men we knew. I mean the night she painted
      her whole body purple
                              and crawled into a party
dragging two bowling balls, bobbing a prick-head of papier-mâché.
                              Now she teaches at the Y,
drives back and forth from the suburbs in the old
      station wagon.
I love her, but it is not the same between us, her thighs
                              like ponds silting
from underneath and glazing over, blue-green with varicose
      algae.
O aging mermaid of the suburbs, I shall teach you Prufrock
                              in Continuing Ed,
and I promise not to embarrass you, to touch you lightly
as the monarch comes to the leaf of the black locust
or the wand of the Channel 4 weatherman touches a distant
      storm.
These nights I think you sleep as the wilderness sleeps beyond
      your windows,
                              anaesthetized,

while the city's nimbus dilates, strewing light
      by the ruined creeks.
                              See how the stag
deer leaps and hesitates and is frozen in the headlights,
      the muskrat tunnels into a covert,
the rabbit works a pink sock into her nest of lespedeza and
      sedge.
No wonder the undertaker plays the harmonica! No wonder
there are psychiatrists everywhere ashamed of their singing!
      No wonder it is always Wednesday.


     4

Old hands crusted over with eczema, otherworldly, cold
                         and blunt as potatoes
on the back of the pew Wednesday nights, where we would go
      to pray,
and all the widows were hungry for God, like debutantes
                      at the end of a boyless summer,
or nun-poets of the Dark Ages singing the sensual body of the
      church.
My grandmother, Mrs. Lyle, Mrs. Patterson, Viola Wilkins,
      Mavis Kent,
and a few others who could still pray, weep, and sing
      unabashedly,
each went down. Each languished in Bobby Summerford's
      rest home
                    in the perversity
of extravagant leisure—game hour, story hour.
      Near their deaths
                    not one of them believed

any man had walked on the moon. I am not concerned that
    they rot
sealed away from us, distant as the death of grocery chickens.
On the news there is a fly-bait hand extending
    from the rubble.
                  I know, a man's hand,
hand of a believer in Allah. Some nights I dream that I am
    lost,
wandering among numberless houses, dangling like a root in a
    sewer.
One of my hands is rotting; I keep it in my shirt like
    Napoleon's hand.
This is that season, decadence in the leaf we look at. We sing
                  for the safe eggs,
sing with the iced fish in the Piggly Wiggly, the worms, the
    pale grass,
and the moon seems, yes, to sing, and the water sings in the
    spigot.
The old furniture sings mildew and mold, and I am happy
with my friends who remember a few jokes and are serious
                  at other times,
and with my friends who are at once joking and serious,
and with the most serious jokes, the music of Mozart and
    Brahms.


    5

I think of the mayfly, who in adulthood forms perfect genitalia
                  but no stomach,
who lives for a single day to fly up and lay her eggs in the
    branches

of one of those willows that grow on small islands
      in the Tennessee River,
and I think of the fishermen, close by when the smallmouth
      gather
to wait for the end of the flight, when the exhausted come
      home.

*Transparent Gestures* (1989)

# TRANSPARENT GESTURES

There is in the human voice
A quavery vowel sometimes,
More animal than meaning,
More mineral than gentle,

A slight nuance by which my
Mother would recognize lies,
Detect scorn or envy, sober
Things words would not admit,

Though it's true the best liars
Must never know they lie.
They move among goodbyes
Worded like congratulations

We listen for and hear until
Some misery draws us back
To what it really was they
Obviously meant not to say.

And misery often draws us
Out to meadows or trees,
That speechless life where
Everything inhuman is true.

Mother spoke for tentative
People, illiterate, unsure.
To think of it her way is to
Reduce all words to tones

The wind might make anytime
With a few dead leaves. Our
Own names called in the dark
Or quail rising. Sounds that

Go straight from the ear to
The heart. There all the time,
They are a surface too clear
To see. Written down, no

Matter how right, they are too
Slow and vain as those soft
Vows we spoke in childhood to
Wild things, birds or rabbits

We meant to charm. When
Mother mentioned oaks,
They could be cut down, sawn
Into boards and nailed together

As rooms, and she was mostly
Quiet, standing in the kitchen,
Her pin rolling like law
Across plains of biscuit dough

While dark ripened, wind
Died on the tongue of each leaf.
The night broke in pieces
If she cleared her throat.

# ONE OF THE CITIZENS

What we have here is a mechanic who reads Nietzsche,
who talks of the English and the French Romantics
as he grinds the pistons; who takes apart the Christians
as he plunges the tarred sprockets and gummy bolts
into the mineral spirits that have numbed his fingers;
an existentialist who dropped out of school to enlist,
who lied and said he was eighteen, who gorged himself
all afternoon with cheese and bologna to make the weight
and guarded a Korean hill before he roofed houses,
first in East Texas, then here in North Alabama. Now
his work is logic and the sure memory of disassembly.
As he dismantles the engine, he will point out damage
and use, the bent nuts, the worn shims of uneasy agreement.
He will show you the scar behind each ear where they
put in the plates. He will tap his head like a kettle
where the shrapnel hit, and now history leaks from him,
the slow guile of diplomacy and the gold war makes,
betrayal at Yalta and the barbed wall circling Berlin.
As he sharpens the blades, he will whisper of Ruby and Ray.
As he adjusts the carburetors, he will tell you
of finer carburetors, invented in Omaha, killed by Detroit,
of deals that fall like dice in the world's casinos,
and of the commission in New York that runs everything.
Despiser of miracles, of engineers, he is as drawn
by conspiracies as his wife by the gossip of princesses,
and he longs for the definitive payola of the ultimate fix.
He will not mention the fiddle, though he played it once
in a room where farmers spun and curses were flung,

or the shelter he gouged in the clay under the kitchen.
He is the one who married early, who marshaled a crew
of cranky half-criminal boys through the incompletions,
digging ditches, setting forms for culverts and spillways
for miles along the right-of-way of the interstate;
who moved from construction to Goodyear Rubber
when the roads were finished; who quit each job because
he could not bear the bosses after he had read Kafka;
who, in his mid-forties, gave up on Sartre and Camus
and set up shop in this Quonset hut behind the welder,
repairing what comes to him, rebuilding the small engines
of lawnmowers and outboards. And what he likes best
is to break it all down, to spread it out around him
like a picnic, and to find not just what's wrong
but what's wrong and interesting—some absurd vanity,
or work, that is its own meaning—so when it's together
again and he's fired it with an easy pull of the cord,
he will almost hear himself speaking, as the steel
clicks in the single cylinder, in a language almost
like German, clean and merciless, beyond good and evil.

# THE SADNESS OF EARLY AFTERNOONS

Maybe the Sheikh gets to toss his oil wells in the dice,
But here in the living room it's wan more than warm,
After coffee and sweet rolls, when the vacuum groans
Ahead of her like a troll, and life is longer than she
Thought in high school, and time is the critical dust
That floats above the stereo before the kids return.
She buffs her nails or plucks from her domestic well
A flaccid cup of Metrecal, and irons while the TV unfolds
An evolving plot that is less like a line than a tree,
With each pictured life stretching its fabulous branch:
Blackmail, divorce, passion in caves, prisons, gazebos,
Dead-ending into the pink bud of each commercial. Soaps
Are all like this, playing out the reel of eventualities,
Each unlikely trope securing fate in the continuing
Episode. The girl who scoured sinks and polished crystal
In the Emersons' kitchen had money. She slowly sank in.
She was someone from the past, which will come later.
But when it comes, the answers only pose more questions.
Will the chauffeur be sent back to Poland? What object,
Yet unseen, spread that mortifying shock on Erica's face?
Was it Chad or Josh?—these names that call to the unborn.
And there are séances where poverty speaks to good fortune.
There are so many deep gazes, cryptic sighs, and far away
The new actress muttering into the mystery of the telephone;
So many doctors in trouble for something that is not quite
Clear, some miswielded scalpel or drunken ambiguous procedure . . .
The past is everything, though for now, all that may be seen
Is a soliloquy, the particulars of which will not be fully

Comprehended until next week, when Lance returns from Salvador,
Making Jessica erotically glad, but throwing the whole gilded
Household of the Kenwoods, those sourpuss Episcopalians,
A curve of destitution, and then the scene changes: a blond
Girl we do not know yet is struggling up a seaside hill.
The sense is incomplete, though we can guess why Ashley,
Our helpless and innocent Rapunzel, is pawning the rubies.
And it *is* like life, where the leading cause of infidelity
Is amnesia, with every plot carried out and entered into
The rec room of the veterans' hospital, into the contiguous
Gravy of days that are plotless for the unemployed,
The unemployable, when the last food stamps have been
Thrown into the ante in the impossible bluff on a straight,
And the ace of obsessions has gone unplayed—except here
On the box. It is not that we do not know what will happen,
But how will it happen? What unforeseeable kink
Will draw the dead back up into the camera's glyptic eye?
And who will tell Gerard, caught in that far set: that
Child, the one you thought was yours, was never yours,
And you yourself are not who you think you are. Already
Tomorrow's table is being set for another guest, some hot
Latin fluff or venerable tabloid star to be written in
As you are written off. And this is what has been held back:
The prognosis, the story beneath that new bandage and lump,
Is like the exegesis you were always too ready to accept,
Not understanding what we ... if only we, out here, could come
Into the story and tell you ... that night you were run down
And lay unconscious, the doctor who operated was not drunk,
But bought off by Kirsten, your own wife, who conspired
With your unknown brother, the Sheikh. And that procedure
That would reverse everything, bring you roaring out of

The wheelchair, has been discovered already, but will be
Used against you in the end, perhaps because our desire
Is that you join us here in the suburbs and the projects,
In Peoria and Schenectady. In the vast harem boredom keeps,
We are offering you the sinlessness of our own unlived lives.

# ON THE BEARING OF WAITRESSES

Always I thought they suffered, the way they huffed
through the Benzedrine light of waffle houses,
hustling trays of omelets, gossiping by the grill,
or pruning passes like the too prodigal buds of roses,
and I imagined each come home to a trailer court,
the yard of bricked-in violets, the younger sister
pregnant and petulant at her manicure, the mother
with her white Bible, the father sullen in his corner.
Wasn't that the code they telegraphed in smirks?
And wasn't this disgrace, to be public and obliged,
observed like germs or despots about to be debunked?
Unlikely brides, apostles in the gospel of stereotypes,
their future was out there beyond the parked trucks,
between the beer joints and the sexless church,
the images we'd learned from hayseed troubadours—
perfume, grease, and the rending of polarizing loves.
But here in the men's place, they preserved a faint
decorum of women and, when they had shuffled past us,
settled in that realm where the brain approximates
names and rounds off the figures under uniforms.
Not to be honored or despised, but to walk as spies would,
with almost alien poise in the imperium of our disregard,
to go on steadily, even on the night of the miscarriage,
to glide, quick smile, at the periphery of appetite.
And always I had seen them listening, as time brought
and sent them, hovering and pivoting as the late
orders turned strange, *blue garden, brown wave.* Spit
in the salad, wet socks wrung into soup, and this happened.
One Sunday morning in a truckstop in Bristol, Virginia,

a rouged and pancaked half-Filipino waitress
with hair dyed the color of puffed wheat and mulberries
singled me out of the crowd of would-be bikers
and drunken husbands guzzling coffee to sober up
in time to cart their disgusted wives and children
down the long street to the First Methodist Church.
Because I had a face she trusted, she had me wait
that last tatter of unlawful night that hung there
and hung there like some cast-off underthing
caught on the spikes of a cemetery's wrought-iron fence.
And what I had waited for was no charm of flesh,
not the hard seasoning of luck, or work, or desire,
but all morning, in the sericea by the filthy city lake,
I suffered her frightened lie, how she was wanted
in Washington by the CIA, in Vegas by the FBI—
while time shook us like locks that would not break.
And I did not speak, though she kept pausing to look
back across one shoulder, as though she were needed
in the trees, but waxing her slow paragraphs into
chapters, filling the air with her glamour and her shame.

# THE KITCHEN GODS

Carnage in the lot: blood freckled the chopping block—
The hen's death is timeless, frantic.
Its numbskull lopped, one wing still drags
The pointless circle of a broken clock,
But the vein fades in my grandmother's arm on the ax.
The old ways fade and do not come back.
The sealed aspirin does not remember the willow.
The supermarket does not remember the barnyard.
The hounds of memory come leaping and yapping.
One morning is too large to fit inside the mouth.
My grandmother's life was a long time
Toiling between Blake's root-and-lightning
Yahweh and the girlish Renaissance Christ
That plugged the flue in her kitchen wall.
Early her match flamed across the carcass.
Her hand, fresh from the piano, plunged
The void bowel and set the breadcrumb heart.
The stove's eye reddened. The day's great spirit rose
From pies and casseroles. That was the house—
Reroofed, retiled, modernized, and rented out,
It will not glide up and lock among the stars.
The tenants will not find the pantry fully stocked
Or the brass boat where she kept the matches dry.
I find her stone and rue our last useless
Divisive arguments over the divinity of Christ.
Only where the religion goes on without a god
And the sandwich is wolfed down without a blessing,

I think of us bowing at the table there:
The grand patriarch of the family holding forth
In staunch prayer, and the potato pie I worshiped.
The sweeter the pie, the shorter the prayer.

# MULE

Here is this horse from a bad family, hating his burden and snaffle,
>     not patient
So much as resigned to his towpath around the sorghum mill, but
>     pawing the grist,
Laying back his missile ears to balk, so the single spoke of his wheel
>     freezes, the gears lock.
Not sad, but stubborn, his temperament is tolerance, though his voice,
Old door aching on a rusty hinge, blasts the martins from their
>     gourds, and he would let
Nothing go behind him: the speckled hen, the green world his
>     blinders magnify.
With the heel of one ecclesiastical hoof, he would stun goats or gods.

Half-ass, garrulous priest, his religion's a hybrid appetite that feasts
>     on contradictions.
In him Jefferson dreamed the end of slavery and endless fields, but
>     the labor goes on
In prefabricated barns, by stalled regiments of canopied tractors,
>     in offices
Where the harvest is computed to the least decimal point, to the last
>     brown bowl of wheat.
Not with him, the soil yields and futures swell into the radio.
His place, finally, is to be loved as a curiosity, as an art almost dead,
>     like this sulfurous creek
Of molasses he brings oozing down from the bundles of cane.

Sometimes in the library I pause suddenly and think of the mule,
    desiring, perhaps, some lost sweetness,
Some fitful husk or buttercup that blooms wildly beyond the margins.
Such a peace comes over the even rows, the bound volumes where
    the unicorn
Bows his unearthly head, where the horned gods of fecundity rear in
    the pages of the sun.
All afternoon I will think of the mule's dignity, of his shrunken lot—
While the statistics slip the tattered net of my attention,
While the lullabies erect their precise nests in the footnotes.

I like to think of the silver one of my childhood and the dark red
    one, Red.
Avuncular, puritanical, he stands on hooves as blue as quarries,
And I think his is the bray I have held back all of my life, in churches
Where the offering passed discreetly from one laborer to the next, in
    the factories of sleep,
Plunging a greased hand into the vat of mineral spirits.
And I think I have understood nothing better than the mule's cruelty
    and petty meanness:
How, subjugated, he will honk his incomparable impudence; stop for
    no reason;
Or, pastured with inferiors, stomp a newborn calf on a whim.

This is the mule's privilege: not to be governed badly by lashes, nor to
    be turned
Easily by praise; but, sovereign of his own spirit, to take his own time,
To meditate in the hardening compost under the rotting collars.
To sleep in wet straw. To stand for nothing but himself.
In August he will stand up to his withers in the reeking pond. In the
    paradise of mules

He will stand with the old cows, contemplative, but brooding a little
over the sores in his shoulders,
Remembering the dull shoes of the cultivator and the jet heads of the
mowing machine.
Being impotent and beautiful, he will dream of his useless romances.

# THE FOOLISHNESS

After his last brindled half-Guernsey had been sold off,
after the third accident in two months, when we hid
the keys and jerked the starter from the blue Dodge,
and long after the first heart attack in the hayfield,
without mentioning it to anyone, my grandfather began
collecting plastic milk jugs and storing them in his barn,
stuffing the gunnysacks, laying whiteness down the aisle
where the halters hung like dim frames of photographs
and the hens' speckled scat whirled in cotillions of dust.
Before that he'd kept an archive of superannuated tools,
severed belts, odd linkages, screws with stripped threads,
as though, given time, the swaddling crud would unwind
from the brittle gears, the transmission frozen in reverse
would bolt the tractor forward through the unturned fields.
Or these jugs would hold other than what they'd held:
honeyed things of the spirit, bleached Saharas of wheat,
water to stanch fire, or ballast to float us past the flood.
Not that he ever slowed for fear, nor did he often
pause, cankering into dream. His wisdom was classical
and practical: to drive staples cross-grain to hold
the wire, to keep cows with small heads for easy birthing.
Sisyphus of farms, he knew the husk that transcends use
and teetered in a snaggle of plows where the spiders
were tracking rust onto the seat of the cultivator
from the upward-turning teeth of the harrow. Ahead,
morning tore at the fresh webs, the ghosts of picksacks
swayed in the crooked balance of the broken scale,
and before dawn roused the engines, he would come in secret,
with more absence than he could possibly have drunk,

bringing up from the dump, like a boy's stolen melons
or the effigies of pigs, his jugs of Pet and Meadow Gold,
building altars in troughs, raising monuments in the stable
where Charlie, the elderly gelding, had fallen and was shot.
And even when my father found them and told him
and told him, and explained again, he would not stop,
but continued, more stubbornly then, filling the loft,
rattling in the crib's musical shucks, so the field mouse
turned back from the least kernel of the spindliest cob,
and when the pigeons broke from their nests in the rafters
with a bilious cooing and a gallows laughter of wings,
he might have thought he heard the future come suddenly,
as though the gate above him would open that easily,
completing the foolishness, and he must have known
the ancient lie of form, the empty truth of containers.

# WINTER RETREAT:
## HOMAGE TO MARTIN LUTHER KING, JR.


There is a hotel in Baltimore where we came together,
we black and white educated and educators,
for a week of conferences, for important counsel
sanctioned by the DOE and the Carter administration,
to make certain difficult inquiries, to collate notes
on the instruction of the disabled, the deprived,
the poor, who do not score well on entrance tests,
who, failing school, must go with mop and pail
skittering across the slick floors of cafeterias,
or climb dewy girders to balance high above cities,
or, jobless, line up in the bone cold. We felt
substantive burdens lighten if we stated it right.
Very delicately, we spoke in turn. We walked
together beside the still waters of behaviorism.
Armed with graphs and charts, with new strategies
to devise objectives and determine accountability,
we empathetic black and white shone in seminar rooms.
We enunciated every word clearly and without accent.
We moved very carefully in the valley of the shadow
of the darkest agreement error. We did not digress.
We ascended the trunk of that loftiest cypress
of Latin grammar the priests could never
successfully graft onto the rough green chestnut
of the English language. We extended ourselves
with that sinuous motion of the tongue that is half
pain and almost eloquence. We black and white
politely reprioritized the parameters of our agenda
to impact equitably on the Seminole and the Eskimo.

We praised diversity and involvement, the sacrifices
of fathers and mothers. We praised the next white
Gwendolyn Brooks and the next black Robert Burns.
We deep made friends. In that hotel we glistened
over the *pommes au gratin* and the *poitrine de veau*.
The morsels of lamb flamed near where we talked.
The waiters bowed and disappeared among the ferns.
And there is a bar there, there is a large pool.
Beyond the tables of the drinkers and raconteurs,
beyond the hot tub brimming with Lebanese tourists
and the women in expensive bathing suits doing laps,
if you dive down four feet, swim out far enough,
and emerge on the other side, it is sixteen degrees.
It is sudden and very beautiful and colder
than thought, though the air frightens you at first,
not because it is cold, but because it is visible,
almost palpable, in the fog that rises from difference.
While I stood there in that cheek-numbing snow,
all Baltimore was turning blue. And what I remember
of that week of talks is nothing the record shows,
but the revelation outside, which was the city
many came to out of the fields, then the thought
that we had wanted to make the world kinder,
but, in speaking proudly, we had failed a vision.

# PUSSY

Not yet have I seen it published in 18-point bold.
Neither in the British nor the American anthologies.

When I say it I feel the soul of fairness and feminism
About to descend precipitately, lift me by the scruff
Of the occiput, and drop me like a clam on a rock.

I feel the preachers and Aunt Pollys of the world
Approaching with their portable altars and soap.

Long ago my mother told me write uplifting things.

But five black boys smuggled it across the bottoms
From the bootlegger's hut and slipped it in my ear—

Reuben, Clifford, Roman, Joe, and Alphonso Lemon.
I had no idea, I am very sure, what it could mean.

I thought the fishy condoms lovers had flung into ditches
Were the hog bladders my uncles had used for balls,
Scuffling and roughhousing in the lot behind the barn
Twenty-five or thirty years before I was born.

But even then I must have known it was wrong.

I was pulling a stunted bluegill from a scummy hole
In that creek everyone in my family likes to mention
Over and over because it goes by our family name,
If it goes at all, frothing the ooze of dairy farms.

Just then the five Lemons came hooting and hollering
And crowded in around me with their long poles.

I had not seen them before. I knew who they were.

Long ago my grandfather's grandfather took the ferry
Across the Tennessee River and brought back Reba,
Their grandmother's grandmother. She had been sold
To a plantation over there for four hundred dollars,
And he had to jaw two hours and feign lust for another,
Lighter girl to get her back for four hundred dollars.

Everyone in my family tells this story over and over
As though we had all crossed the river Jordan and
Jehovah himself stood waiting in a white cotton robe.

That day long ago we boys lifted dozens from the hole,
Fussing though, for they kept saying it over and over.

Many times since, privately, I have spoken it in love,
But not until today have I written it down on paper,
So I remembered the fish and the history of that woman.

Even if I have told it badly, being a man. I know
The scrawniest women were worth more than the strongest men.

# EVERY DAY THERE ARE NEW MEMOS

Fact-fluffed, appended with dates, they drift down, O bountiful
    accountings, O grim disbursements!
I take them from the box. I take them from the groggy hand that
    moved for no more purpose
Than to record the slow minutes of meetings where nothing was
    really resolved,
But I keep thinking that those names hoisted above small towns
    and splashed
With orange paint across the silver tanks of water towers
Mark the final defeat of the block plant and the soybean fields, and
    I keep believing
That those luminous nicknames, Blade and Superstar, as they surface
    in Queens or the South Bronx—
Spraypainted so artfully on the sides of subway cars that one
Has to look two or three times beneath curiosity and admiration to
    make out the lettering—
Represent our surest victories over glass, concrete, and steel.

In a time of vague and courteous doubt, in the quantum amnesia, in
    the fretful face
Of failed loves, I have put my faith in the locally signed work:
    John Payne
Hardware, Red Mullins Rebuilt and Guaranteed Transmissions,
    Bob and Stump Stevenson
Of Stevenson Brothers Furniture. Everywhere else the family business
    is lost. Everywhere else
The anonymous acme of the great purchase rewards and subsumes all
    minor concerns,

Subcontracting for its own name a tone: soporific, indigenous to no
    tongue,
But projecting a gray aura of confidence, of accurate machines.
That is why I work very hard to make out the name Delray Jenks
    under the Prudential sign.
I imagine him sneaking out at night in his old shoes to repossess his
    city with paint,
Writing soliloquies on sidewalks, aphorisms in public restrooms—

But we do not truly read them, the entries are so profligate they
    seem cracks
Ramifying up walls, flawing the marble patina of our days.
Yet in just this dubious way the leopard and the fox express their
    clear boundaries,
The braggart signals to the saint from across the abyss.
Whatever was brought low is lifted high. Whatever was nameless shines.
The insides of buses are like phonebooks listing the fierce and the
    promiscuous,
And in the woods, the lovers who carve their initials deep
Into the beeches are like Whitman reviewing his own poetry. Proud flesh,
Proud glamour of the self, my joy now is to sign this openly, I who
    often wanted to be no one
And dreaded more than stitches the roll approaching my name.

# CARPE DIEM

Though pretty, it rarely worked, lining seduction
with worms or being always right, like some ideal
marvel of professors, when there was time for music,
which was never words so much as time. And the subject
of those songs we prayed all adolescence to become
was not love, really, but the loneliness love betrays:
summers immersed in childhood's various waters,
warm and cool springs weaving the plaid of Brushy Lake,
and letting it all go, that guilty underwater rush.
Such easy idylls as the ice cream truck interrupts
are what we have of abandon, though we would not leave.
Even while we were there, we were begging to return,
and some of the bodies springing from bumpered posts
had already grown breasts, strange hairs at the groin
like cursive signatures we had once itched to sign.
To speak of the body is to return to that very place
where the body was most alive, not to the corpse.
Those who think of bodies most haven't seen one,
not yet. While they endure the first hormonal surge,
their bodies answer even dreams with awkward thrusts
that seem to catch them in machines and hurt memory.
And they still harbor toys: stuffed animals forgetting
their names, incomplete sets, trucks with broken grilles.
Only their guarded silences seem unseasonably adult,
though each door stonewalls the moment of flesh
until the chrysalis breaks and they fall to each other.
In lachrymose spasms. In ripe seizures of abstract joy.
Still, I don't remember what hurt me most, the blue
and womanly corpse or the slim body of my first girl.

Perhaps because the corpse was family, in my mind
it seemed to surprise some shameful act of bestial love
that stuck the eyes on open. As for the girl,
since she lay in a half-dark back seat and cringed
a little out of childish modesty, I cannot swear I saw
the breasts embarking, the slow gift of the thighs,
but staggered afterward from the car and sat a good
twenty minutes on a rock, drunk on nothing but sense
and alien fortune. I saw us married and quarrelsome
in a trailer beside the silo on her family's dairy farm,
and then, faintly, the edge of a harder embrace,
skull against cheek, ribcage against breast. The sky
wore that raincloud look of a poorly rinsed wound.
Both times attach me to a third and ring like a chord.
I grieved them both and loved steadily as I grieved,
but why do they come together now, corpse and girl?
—admonishing me, *Be quick and gentle as you change
seat to bed, sheet to shroud,* as though I were not
already all here and late maybe for the time of my life.

# A BLASPHEMY

A girl attacked me once with a number 2 Eagle pencil
for a whiny lisping impression of a radio preacher
she must have loved more than sophistication or peace,
for she took the pencil in a whitened knuckle
and drove the point with all her weight behind it
through a thick pair of jeans, jogging it at the end
and twisting it so the lead broke off under the skin,
an act undertaken so suddenly and dramatically
it was as though I had awakened in a strange hotel
with sirens going off and half-dressed women rushing
in every direction with kids tucked under their arms;
as though the Moslems had retaken Jerusalem for
the twelfth time, the crusaders were riding south,
and the Jews in Cádiz and Granada were packing
their bags, mapping the snowy ghettos of the north.
But where we were, it was still Tuscaloosa, late
summer, and the heat in her sparsely decorated room
we had come to together after work was so miserable
and intense the wallpaper was crimping at each seam,
the posters of daisies and horses she had pasted up
were fallen all over the floor. Whatever I thought
would happen was not going to happen. Nothing
was going to happen with any of the three billion women
of the world forever. The time it would take
for the first kindness was the wait for a Campbellite
to accept Darwin and Galileo or for all Arkansas
to embrace a black Messiah. The time it would take
for even a hand to shyly, unambiguously brush my own
was the years Bertrand Russell waited for humanism,

disarmament, and neutrality. And then she was
there, her cloth daubing at the darkly jellying wound.
In contrition, she bowed with tweezers to pick the grit.
With alcohol, she cleansed the rubbery petals.
She unspooled the white gauze and spread the balm of mercy.
Because she loved Christ, she forgave me. And what
was that all about? I wondered, walking home
through the familiar streets, the steeple of each church
raised like a beneficent weapon, the mark of the heretic
on my thigh, and mockery was still the unforgivable sin.

## PASTORAL FOR DERRIDA

When coyotes hunt, they come as a clean silence
comes to a text. They come from beyond myths
out of the tree line along the creek and pick
a lamb, a tender and easy word. Spoken once,
it won't be changed, and the ewe bawls all day.
All night under flocculent covers, we give her up
to sleep. The next morning, clear and warm,
the sun's a word we'd want to mean happiness,
but the ewe holds her place, perfecting rage,
and lets the burrs knot her wool, and goes down
wobbly on scuffed hocks, muddy with grief.
The cry swells deep in her hot sheep heart
and floats out to us like pieces of her lamb,
spleen and scruff, follicles pebbly as toads,
so we see, not just lamb, but our own kids
that perishable, that liable to be broken on fangs.
Like any parent, I'd think too much of peril.
My worries blur from the herd of likelihood,
far from the soft, hospitable centers of dens,
where the lawnmower throws a shrapnel of wire,
where the deaf missile strays from the silo.
Still, I wonder who or what she means to call—
not us, certainly, any more than clouds or trees—
or if the petition, repeating, means at all,
or is some hunger that longs beyond capacity
of stomachs, with no object in grain or grass.
It could be any thing or one, sheep or man:
in elms, summer squalls or winter whines;
the cat howls on the barbed, necessary prick.

The times I'd cry all day, I finally was the cry
itself and not myself, but sob on lemony sob
like wave on wave breaking against a rock,
autonomous, purer once there were no tears.
Any cry begins profound, in the ore of words,
in the lungs' pink lode and honeycomb. It
thickens like gravity in the unsuckled udder.
Hear it, and you'd know the theme was loss,
or how every cry's a compass with no needle
that offers, anyway, some vague direction,
as the disbeliever offers up his prayer
to the crazed heavens, to the absent gods.
And surely even the ewe must know
it does no good to cry, to carry this tune
until it carries her—"to the dogs," we'd say,
to butcher and marl. Neither does it help
to ply the tools of facile affection, sweet
words that would succor, hands that would
soothe the hives of demonstrative afflictions,
though these mean well. Poor culpable
spirit, unreckoning Dostoevski among the beasts—
I would stand, too, and send each
bleat like a shovel into the flinty air
under the hermeneutical circle of the vulture.

# LIFE OF SUNDAYS

Down the street, someone must be praying, and though I don't
Go there anymore, I want to at times, to hear the diction
And the tone, though the English pronoun for God is obsolete—

What goes on is devotion, which wouldn't change if I heard:
The polished sermon, the upright's arpeggios of vacant notes.
What else could unite widows, bankers, children, and ghosts?

And those faces are so good as they tilt their smiles upward
To the rostrum that represents law, and the minister who
Represents God beams like the white palm of the good hand

Of Christ raised behind the baptistry to signal the multitude,
Which I am not among, though I feel the abundance of calm
And know the beatitude so well I do not have to imagine it,

Or the polite old ones who gather after the service to chat,
Or the ritual linen of Sunday tables that are already set.
More than any other days, Sundays stand in unvarying rows

That beg attention: there is that studied verisimilitude
Of sanctuary, so even mud and bitten weeds look dressed up
For some eye in the distant past, some remote kingdom

Where the pastures are crossed by thoroughly symbolic rivers.
That is why the syntax of prayers is so often reversed,
Aimed toward the dead who clearly have not gone ahead

But returned to prior things, a vista of angels and sheep,
A desert where men in robes and sandals gather by a tree.
Hushed stores, all day that sense a bell is about to ring—

I recognized it, waking up, before I weighed the bulk of news
Or saw Saturday night's cars parked randomly along the curb,
And though I had no prayer, I wanted to offer something

Or ask for something, perhaps out of habit, but as the past
Must always be honored unconsciously, formally, and persists
On this first and singular day, though I think of it as last.

*Apocalyptic Narrative*
*and Other Poems* (1993)

# THE WORK OF POETS

Willie Cooper, what are you doing here, this early in your death?

To show us what we are, who live by twisting words—
Heaven is finished. A poet is as anachronistic as a blacksmith.

You planted a long row and followed it. Signed your name X for
    seventy years.
Poverty is not hell. Fingers cracked by frost
And lacerated by Johnson grass are not hell.

Hell is what others think we are.

You told me once, "Never worry."
Your share of worry was as small as your share of the profits,

Mornings-after of lightning and radiator shine,
The beater Dodge you bought in late October—
By February, its engine would hang from a rafter like a ham.

You had a free place to stay, a wife
Who bore you fourteen children. Nine live still.

You live in the stripped skeleton of a shovelbill cat.

Up here in the unforgivable amnesia of libraries,
Where many poems lie dying of first-person omniscience,
The footnotes are doing their effete dance, as always.

But only one of your grandsons will sleep tonight in Kilby Prison.
The hackberry in the sand field will be there long objectifying.

Once I was embarrassed to have to read for you
A letter from Shields, your brother in Detroit,
A hick-grammared, epic lie of northern women and money.

All I want is to get one grain of the dust to remember.

I think it was your advice I followed across the oceans.
What can I do for you now?

# THE BRIDGE

These fulsome nouns, these abbreviations of the air,
Are not real, but two of them may fit a small man
I knew in high school who, seeing an accident,
Stopped one day, leapt over a mangled guardrail,
Took a mother and two children from a flooded creek,
And lifted them back to the world. In the dark,
I do not know, there is no saying, but he pulled
Them each up a tree, which was not the tree of life
But a stooped Alabama willow, flew three times
From the edge of that narrow bridge as though
From the selfless shore of a miracle, and came back
To the false name of a real man, Arthur Peavahouse.
He could sink a set shot from thirty feet. One night
I watched him field a punt and scat behind a wall
Of blockers like a butterfly hovering an outhouse.
He did not love the crashing of bodies. He
Did not know that mother and her three children
But went down one huge breath to their darkness.
There is no name for that place, you cannot
Find them following a white chain of bubbles
Down the muddy water of these words. But I saw
Where the rail sheared from the bridge—which is
Not real since it was replaced by a wider bridge.
Arthur Peavahouse weighed a hundred and twenty pounds.
Because he ran well in the broken field, men
Said he was afraid. I remember him best
At a laboratory table, holding a test tube
Up to the light, arranging equations like facts,
But the school is air over a parking lot. You

Are too far from that valley for it to come
All the way true, although it is not real.
Not two miles from that bridge, one afternoon
In March, in 1967, one of my great-uncles,
Clyde Maples, a farmer and a commissioner of roads,
And his neighbor, whose name I have forgotten,
Pulled more than a hundred crappies off three
Stickups in that creek—though the creek is not
Real and the valley is a valley of words. You
Would need Clyde Maples to find Arthur Peavahouse,
And you would need Clyde Maples' side yard
Of roadgraders and bulldozers to get even part
Of Clyde Maples, need him like the crappies
Needed those stickups in the creek to tell them
Where they were. Every spring that creek
Darkens with the runoff of hog lots and barns,
Spreading sloughs, obscuring sorghum and corn.
On blind backwater full schoolbuses roll
Down buried roads. Arthur Peavahouse was smart
To run from the huge tackles and unthinking
To throw himself into that roiling water
And test the reality of his arms and his lungs.
Many times I have thought everything I have said
Or thought was a lie, moving some blame or credit
By changing a name, even the color of a lip or bush,
But whenever I think of the lie that stands for truth,
I think of Arthur Peavahouse, and not his good name,
But his deciding, as that car settled to the bottom,
To break free and live for at least one more moment
Upward toward light and the country of words
While the other child, the one he could not save,
Shrugged behind him in the unbreakable harness.

# GRAND PROJECTION

Its huge numbers include us, our cars, houses, and substantial goods,
      but the numbers
Do not stop north of Lake George or south of the Rio Grande.
There is a large number that stands for the Atlantic.
There is a very large number that stands for the Pacific.
Last winter a number of Mexicans smuggling their muscles north in a
      shut railway car
Suffocated and was added to a larger number, which includes the
      teenage pregnancy and whooping crane,
And will it be enough, when the great condor and sea tortoise have
      shrunken to one,
To weigh the hour of ovulation against the bounty of the sperm?

It is not just the children to come. Also, the rat, the opossum, the
      raccoon, and the mourning dove
Have traveled the sewer main and, dead, mounted sufficient work
To be counted among the problems, which include the Mexicans,
      the Ethiopians, and acid rain.
Our problems are so numerous, it is very essential that we count
The boats, their size and type, and the number of life preservers, fire
      extinguishers, and horns.
And it must be clear, even to the forgotten and almost extinct Arapaho,
Why one of us must keep the books of the crows and the ledgers of
      the bees,
And, glumly, another counts the instruments after the failed operation
      as the final
Number is wired to the big toe, and the hands are crossed neatly.

Otherwise, the dark vector keeps on rising on that unlined graph, and
    we feel,
From far south, across the plunging of that gulf, in cities uncharmable
    and vast,
Those streets where a number of the just deceased are left to rot—
There is no telling when the government trucks will come and pick up
    a token number,
No reckoning how many each of the deceased has disappointed,
How many children, crippled, clever, gifted, how many cooperative
    and uncooperative sexual partners.
The unnumbered fruits rot, unprofitable, shameful;
The coat of paint is left to peel, no command is given to recover it, and
    there is nothing to say
After the mortar attack, when the reporters go like maggots, working
    the torn nests.

Or if there is a story, say it was too much to say even a single palm tree,
    the shade of the mission
Where the old one-legged man cut tires into sandals,
Or those bluest of lakes cupped in the craters of dead volcanoes.
Say there were too many saints and holidays, too many small people
Following donkeys up roads that vanished into gullies and trees, too
    many siestas.
Say the mathematicians left, the multiplications were so various, and
    there was nothing left to divide.

But record these zeros, ripening on vines beyond the infected wells,
    look carefully
At the mountain devoid of trees, the men passed out on the streets,
And the women bending to irritate their stony rows of corn, for something
Like history is trying to take place in secret meetings and bombs,

Something that does not include us, though we are there in force,
    counting the dead,
And the aid we read of sending underwrites the new resorts we will
    visit perhaps,
When the sense of history is strongest, just after the peace is signed.

# ROMANCE OF THE POOR

The poor people in Springfield go to Dayton to be miserable in style.
They can hug themselves when they lie side by side on the iron cots.
They can luxuriate in one red bean held under the tongue.
For them, a discarded refrigerator crate, tipped on its side and lined
    with plastic bags,
Is the green shore of an island and a palace's velvet halls.
Every morning they check out of the Club St. Vincent de Paul,
And they clump in the warm gusts that scowl up from the sewers.

They can strip the aluminum from gutters as their mothers harvested
    eggs from boxes of straw.
Against that snow that is all edge, they can wobble and careen from
    bumper to lightpole,
Dancing with the parking meter before dying into the hydrant under
    the fire escape.
Deliriously happy, they lift the sweetest and heaviest wine and sink
    down where the metal is warm,
Across from the cafeteria and that other richest trough,
Kingdom of heaven on earth, emerald dumpster of the pizzeria.

What does it matter if I heap treasure from the stick people, far off
    and helpless, fluttering of brown coats?
Their lives are not my life. I come as a tourist to their woe.
But I remember how quickly dark fell, twenty years ago, thumbing
    from Greensboro to Boulder.
I carried one change of clothes, a notebook, and a little more than
    seven dollars,

And I thought I could live by the grace of hippies and priests or,
     failing that,
Prey on park squirrels and the ducks from municipal ponds.

I did not have to go that way. I could have gone on wrestling those big
     sacks of fertilizer
From the co-op's storage bins to the beds of pickup trucks,
Or bludgeoning ice from the front steps of the coliseum,
But I had to get it straight from the black road and the mouth of the
     blue norther.
There is a high ledge under every overpass where you can sleep if it is
     not too cold.
One morning I woke there beside a short man, a carny and ex-con reared
In the Tennessee Industrial School and a dozen foster homes.

We talked a stupid dream of burglary. We committed the crime of
     brotherhood.
Then, hungry and stiff, we trudged up the ramp to a truckstop, where
     he meant
To convince me to knife a man for three hundred dollars locked in a
     drawer.
He said we could get away, we could take any one of those semis
     idling outside that place
Like great buffaloes blowing clouds and clearing their throats.
But I have taken nothing. I have gotten away clean to Illinois.

Tonight the steaks frown up at me through the odor of blood,
And the poor need no help from poems to limp down the alley and up
     into the van.
They glide to Dayton. They check in to the Club St. Vincent de Paul.

Whatever it is, it is not much that makes a man more than a scrap
    of paper
Torn out of a notebook and thrown from the window of a bus,
    but it is more than nothing.
If he holds himself straight up and does not take the life
Next to his own, give him that much. Leave him to his joy.

# THIRTY-ONE FLAVORS OF HOUSES

More than once, the brain dies here, dies on the name
Of a cloud or flower, and the watch is flushed down the toilet;
Marriages are passed from one to another
Like buckets of water at an old-time fire.
And still each spring the premonition bird
Feathers the same nest in the groin.
And still the addresses and the phone numbers fly apart.
The news, with its joyless victims, does not save us.
Love is all becalmed or starts too fitfully
As though God and the stupid heart conspired
To checker each breakfast table with silence,
And often in the early light it is easy to believe
That face that shines forever and never ages,
But the ocean and the trees come to us at night,
And sometimes we look at each other as the ocean
And trees are seen from the comfort of a window,
Behind which all the points have been won or lost
And history shrugs its indifferent shoulders
And walks across the carpet from its bath
Humming the forgetfulness of a popular song,
A song of victims, a song of late courage
We meant to honor once with money and applause.
Oh surely if there were some cause, we would think
To organize communication, transportation, the shipments
Of shelter and food, or go there ourselves
To be martyrs if there were a new Auschwitz to die in.

# AT THE MIRACLE MALL

Are the replacements in? Dove-colored britches, black shirts,
    harbingers of the look
That already brushed past me as I entered by the east gate, like a
    noun searching for a verb,
And walked slowly under the names of unimaginable families, past
    shops where the same immaculate
Fishnet kept sprawling across driftwood sequined with shells,
And the mannequins went on working out the problems of the world.

One of the mannequins had frosted hair and wore braces, another,
    her goldleaf dreadlocks
Skimming the pages of *War and Peace,* exotic tableaus of the
    Scandinavian and Japanese,
Ambassadorial saints of some mythical cultural commonwealth that
    speaks in a British accent
In the United States and talks, on PBS, compulsively,
Of the great heroes and heroines of opera and classical music.

But mainly it's California the windows send, in surfboards and
    dark glasses,
In bikinis strung a season away, in greed's modest future.
On Friday night you would think the world empties there and
    tumbles in a bee-mill
Of inverted weariness and lust, though it is possible, just past the
    Vision Center,
To look straight ahead and greet no one, to move quietly.

And if you stopped as I stopped outside the tuxedo rental, in that space
That is always empty, in that place that is not a place, but domed,
    vaulted, and fountained,
If you walked there, with death still fresh in your thoughts
As a bone needle driven under one nail from the ashes,
And smelled the sweat of the cloggers and the Elvis imitators,

And felt the live swamp dried and buckled beneath you,
And hesitated by Sears and Foot Locker and Pier 1,
You would want all grief to end there.
You would remember the fraud of the château and the lie of the
    cathedral.
You would want great shoes to replace the eyes and beard.

You would want the clove cigarettes and wicker elephants to restore
    the fingers.
You would want a linen suit to stand for the legs and arms.
You would have that mutable god, that prayer to things,
And that religion, whose prophets are actors and salesmen, whose
    scripture is television,
Whose temples bulge with icons disposable as sacrifice.

There was a cardboard woman outside the jewelry store.
Where there had been pain, there was a Japanese car.
Where there was a voice, whole orchestras were shrunken onto disks.
This was where the corridor lapsed down the long banister.
This is what I came to shining in the depths.

That mirror-shard, that glittering grist at the heart.
And then the lot, identical forgetfulness and distraction,

The gray sins, the white depressions and red divorces parked side
     by side,
The rusty gains, the late-model losses, everything waiting to move us
     again,
To ease us back into the traffic with our gifts.

# CONTEMPT

"Lizards," he'd say, dispensing with local men, and then resheath his
    pen and huff back to his drafting table,
A fiber board pristined with vinyl and overhung with the ambiguous,
    linked appendages of maybe a dozen modular lights,
One of which, now, by some unconscionable kink of logic, he'd bring
    screeching down above
His latest renderings of nun-like, mestiza hens I'd named like
    missiles: the Star 5000, the T-100 Egg Machine.

Those days of fruitless scratching on a pad, those nights of Klee and
    Rilke, and what abortifacient labor
Leaves, instead of money, that sense of energy troweled out and
    slapped up, no more than a phrase or two
That sticks, a sketch, no novel, no painting, only time whining
    irrevocably and the feeling
Of events put off or missed: openings, autograph parties — what else?

The grudging knowledge that, even in this, we were lucky: recession
    was on; Vietnam still shipped its dead.
I had the job because a friend knew a friend; he was someone's son:
    a cardiologist or an architect — I never learned.
Except for the boss, Devon, a transplanted Englishman with waxed
    mustache who chain-smoked Virginia Slims and despised
    Americans,
And Gwendolyn, his Phi Beta Kappa secretary, we worked alone in a
    kind of paneled coop they'd rigged

Above a shop that printed invitations and sold used office machines,
    or we'd go out as a team—
Cullman, Springdale, Gainesville—on this particular morning on a
    road just dusted with the season's first snow,
Stravinsky on the stereo, the piny Georgia hills, our usual patter, high
    culture, high art,
And then the building, massive, white, impregnable, our destination
    then, where we'd come to make something,

One of those brochures or tracts that aspire, through much lyrical glut
    and bedazzlement of facts,
To be taken as an article, objective, empirical: four thousand *bons mots*
    of cant replete with scale drawings
And headed "The World's First Totally Integrated Poultry Processing
    Plant." Was that art? Is this?
Embellished in four colors, translated into Dutch, Spanish, and
    Portuguese? That moment when he said it, "Lizards"?

Or later, when the door opened and the stench of bowels, lungs, and
    hearts welled up to us from the line
That we could just now make out through the steam, that first
    denuded glimpse of carcasses shedding slaughter
And strung by the talons as they moved through the faceless maze of
    women as in some gothic laundry
Fellini might have dredged up for the illuminati in heartfelt homage
    to the enduring spirit of Soutine.

Just that moment then, before a big man, someone officious, a plant
    manager or engineer, herded us in,
A handshake, a nod, and saying, "Here, take these," he gave us each a
    bag marked "Sanitation Suit,"

The silly bag-boy hats, the paper coats, and thin latex gloves that now
    we had to haul on as he led us
Through the machines—the stunner, the killer, the plucker, the
    eviscerator, the de-lunger, the stripper, the chiller—

Each with its grisly attendant—those women, those Picassoesque
    smocks bespattered with yellow and red,
That proletarian chorus line, winking, emoting cool or hard-to-get,
    pregnant high school dropouts,
Tattooed grandmothers, chubby peroxide blondes wagging their
    fannies for the wheels.
So I knew, before the word had formed in the brain, before my friend
    had covered his lips with one hand,

And said it in that whisper that frames the sneer and gives it a secret
    eloquence, that it was coming,
Like one drop melting from a high icicle, falling, and spitting against
    a rock, "Lizards"—
And then, though how could any have heard, those women, as though
    in antiphony—what is the word?—words?—
"Sang," "jeered," "hooted," "whistled," "booed," "crowed," "honked,"
    "squawked"?

If you have ever heard five hundred North Georgia women in full-
    throated glory, parodying the morning cacophony of a barnyard
And knew that sound was meant for you, you would know how God
    sometimes
Will call a brother out of the terrible fields, and why the rest of that
    day stands out on the map of days,
Even the chicken teriyaki they served at lunch, and the ride back,
    snow skunking the ridges—our big idea

To name one bird and follow it from the chicken house through the
　　plant, but gently, describing the genius
Of each machine, and on to the grocery store, where, yes, that was it,
　　a young housewife, no, a widow would pick it up,
Bells would ring, a handsome man, the president of the company,
　　we'd say, would step out from behind the frozen dinners,
And present a check, ten thousand dollars, and then—dissolve to
　　dinner—*an idea of tenderness,* we'd call it,

But would it fly? Each day, I'd write, he'd draw. "Lizards," he'd say by
　　way of greeting and goodbye.
Each night at the strip bar in the shopping center, we'd drink on it.
　　"Rilke is greater than Keats."
"Warhol follows naturally from Mondrian, but what I'm after in my
　　work—call it Caravaggio with a gun—
Is riskier, everything exposed between the observation and display";
　　then, "Imagine what it means,

Living in a place like this, loving men—Men?—Reptiles, lizards,
　　slopes!"—
We'd see them crawling from the bathroom to the stools, and then the
　　women would mount them,
Shut their eyes, and grind down hard in that mockery of a dance they
　　do that seems at first
A quote of love's best motions, then just work, then the promise
　　withdrawn, gone, the money and the girl—

Some guys would shrug and grin; others bluster up, throats
　　tightening, fists purpling above the watered gin,
Before the rage guttered in an epithet or joke they'd still be slurring
　　as they stumbled out into the cold.

Some nights we'd stay until the place grew quiet, late, and later,
   a fierce clinking of bottles; now light
Above the steel mills; now voices: dogs, birds. What would become
   of us?

# SHAME THE MONSTERS

It is good, after all, to pause and lick one's genitalia,
To hunch one's shoulders and gag, regurgitating lunch,
To mark one's curb and grass, to bay when the future beckons from
    the nose,
Not to exhaust so much of the present staring into the flat face of a
    machine,
Not to spend so much of the logic and the voice articulating a
    complex whimper of submission,
But to run with a full stomach under the sun, to play in the simple
    water and to wallow oneself dry in the leaves,
To take the teeth in the neck, if it comes to that,
If it comes to little and lean and silent, to take the position of the
    stone, even to hide under the stone,
But not to ride up the spine of the building with the acid scalding the gut,
Not to sit at a long table, wondering
How not to howl when the tall one again personifies the organization,
Speaking of the customs in remote precincts and the manufacture of
    weapons there,
Or the near Edens where the pitted balls fly over the tonsured lawns.

Dear mammals, help me, the argument with flesh is too fierce if it
    outrides time
And shocks numb the stubborn, beautiful muscles of the heart.
See, in the memorial gardens, how even the cry struggles in its trap
    under that black hat like a flower.
In the long rows of tombstones, the ones who were eaten betray
    nothing of the fear that brought them.
And it was their silence that marked them, day after oathless day, until
    they were covered by the silent lawns.

Better to take the mud in the hands and holler for no reason,
  to praise the strange
Alchemy of mud and rain: there is sex; there is food.
It is good to say anything in the spirit of hair and breasts and warm blood,
And not to deny the private knowledge, not to wonder how not to
  speak of death,
And not to deny the knowledge of death, not to invent the silence,
Not to wonder how not to say the words of love.

# AT SUMMERFORD'S NURSING HOME

Like plants in pots, they sit along the wall,
Breached at odd angles, wheelchairs locked,
Or drift in tortoise-calm ahead of doting sons:

Some are still continent and wink at others
Who seem to float in and out of being here,
And one has balked beside the check-in desk—

A jaunty shred of carrot glowing on one lip,
He fumbles a scared hug from each little girl
Among the carolers from the Methodist church

Until two nurses shush him and move him on.
There is a snatch of sermon from the lounge,
And then my fourth-grade teacher washes up,

And someone else—who is it?—nodding the pale
Varicose bloom of his skull: the bald postman,
The butcher from our single grocery store?

Or is that me, graft on another forty years?
Will I become that lump, attached to tubes
That pump in mush and drain the family money?

Or will I be the one who stops it with a gun,
Or, more insensibly, with pills and alcohol?
And would it be so wrong to liberate this one

Who stretches toward me from his bed and moans
Above the constant chlorine of cleaning up
When from farther down the hall I hear the first

Transmogrifying groans: the bestial O and O
Repeating like a mantra that travels long
Roads of nerves to move a sound that comes

And comes but won't come finally up to words,
Not the oldest ones that made the stories go,
Not even *love,* or *help,* or *hurt,* but goodbye

And hello, grandfather, the rest of your life
Coiled around you like a rope, while one by
One, we strange relatives lean to be recognized.

# MOMENT OF WHITMAN

Coming down Sand Mountain, many things moved with me in the
    car, cosmic aphasia after a spat,
A staticky Jonathan Winters tape, *The Best of the Rolling Stones,*
And then I saw them, hatless, ungoverned, decamping from the
    church, a thread that flared to rope
And sprawled across the parking lot and knotted under trees: the bald
    and freshly permed,
Many with dark coats and red ties or matching purses and shoes,
Innocuous farmers with their retinues of fledgling weightlifters,
    maiden aunts of philosophy students,
Ex-coaches of insurance salesmen and guidance counselors,
Architects plotting the aesthetics of Alabama savings & loans, great
    flocculent femme fatales
Trailing the mountainous sexual wonder of sixteen-year-old boys.

Walt Whitman, snow-jobber and cataloguer of American dreams,
    demographer of miracles,
There was just that instant there, I boiled them in one glimpse and
    thought they'd maybe caucused
For a wedding or a death, or did they love the Lord so much they'd come
On Sunday, Wednesday, and now again on Friday afternoon? And
    some of these, too,
I guessed, had formed the mob I'd seen Saturday two weeks before
    that looked so magisterial, stentorian, Greek,
As it uncoiled in a stark festoon of white sheets and dunces' peaks
    toward some vitriolic
Welder's speech against Earl Warren, Satan, the communists, the
    niggers, and the Jews:

Distinguish them singly or mark them in the curve where they began
      to blur
And fade along the piedmont of fescue, Anguses, and machines.


Were these the faces you cheered westward, and numinous bodies, yet
      unpublished in the secret pages of the grass,
Or does the flying vision always fracture on closer inspection of a part?
Another mile of farms, the mountains sank to hills, a sorghum mill, a
      spotted mule
And then, emblazoned on a barn, a painting of a waterfall where,
      later, I would stop
And grip the rail and watch the violent, white, transfiguring stalk of water
That seemed to rear as it drove down and shattered on the rocks and
      clarified beyond
In many little streams that muddled on and vanished in the trees in
      just that way,
I thought, that death might settle into things, and still, father of joy
      and understanding, I didn't leap.
I stood there glowing under the patient faces of the leaves.

# THE PRIVILEGE

That I took the kickoff, feinted, spun twice, sidestepped a tackle, and,
    glorified,
Ran fifty-five yards in the open field before the safety sheared me at
    the knees and I rolled
Down a gully under a barbwire fence and looked up into the sullen,
    algebraic face of a cow;
But, also, that I came from the dermatologist with my brow parched
    by sunlamps and dry ice
And walked the logging road up Cooper Mountain and spoke to trees;
    that my mute hysteria
On bridges, escalators, and telephones ripened gradually into fear;
    that age did not dignify me;
Also, that I risked my fourth year meditating and erecting cities under
    the old house
And stayed there with the rotting wine cask and the brown bottles
    until my head
Bumped against the floor joists and the bus shunted me off to school;
    not just that my long immersion
In ink filled me with visions of invisibility and supernatural powers;
Not just that I addled years, dividing and subtracting, spelling the
    words I already knew;
But, also, that the shy philosopher I plucked from a party in Tuscaloosa
    and squired to New Orleans
Broke down in Pat O'Brien's and I waited for her in the bleached hall
    of the charity ward
And watched the red-haired intern cover the dead indigent with a
    sheet and suffered
His lecture on the epistemological and literary virtues of Ayn Rand;
    that the night

I lugged her through the foggy streets and left her with the Jesuit
     priest still has some truck with me
When I strap my son into the car or push him past the gleaming
     lawns; that it stands with the nights
Of mescaline, the nights of abortions, and the nights of betrayals;
     nothing will shake it
From the totem of my forty-second year, even if I arrive at clarity, with
     some bitter water for the lilies,
With some sweet nitrogen for the willows, for that was the privilege,
     to carry the light itself
And not burn down, not yet, and I will not turn Judas to the madness.

# APOCALYPTIC NARRATIVE

### 1

Clearing the boxes, tins of stale biscuits, powdered eggs
And milk, dried soybeans, we found our last provisions
Whole except for syringes and numbing drugs
Imaginative junkies had stripped from the medical kits.
The water was still pure in each forty-gallon jug,
The U.S. government cheese barely rinded with mold.
Two weeks' rations for ten thousand, the foreman said.
One man hummed. Another told a joke of diddling
A woman so fat he didn't know if it was out or in,
Though none brooked the hotter subject underneath:
The exponential x-ray that would blast all buildings,
Bridges, and trees, or the fine ash, fallen in dreams,
The fever and vomiting, the putrefaction of the skin—
That blind nightmare we fattened for forty years.
It ran with hell. It ended. It was not the world
We took on wobbling dollies, up the steep ledge
Under the bat-fouled bluff, and dumped in the truck,
But strangely disappointing, then, to see the cave
Emptied to darkness and know, too, the whole place
Would go to spiders, the entrance be boarded up,
Though, later, a local dentist established there
A live nativity so popular the church put bleachers up,
And once the fundamentalist governor came and stood
Before us playing a simple shepherd with a crook,
Commemorating hope. The mountain overhead, five
Hundred million tons of limestone, was not enough.

## 2

Too much of the trappings of our imagined ends
Depends on the hoax and rot of lapsed mythologies,
Horned broodstock of the dreamlife, ghosts
Of some earlier holiness, wisdomed up from warnings
And grafted onto laws already weighted down
With ancient torts, preferments, property rights—
But the dream believes most what logic denies:
Those crusty gods, those fires that gut the heart.
When I was a boy in Alabama, I loved my mother's
Biscuits, March rain pelleting on the tin roof,
My crippled, one-eyed dog; but feared the dark,
The snaky pond, the neighbor kid who'd come
On stormy nights and hunker just beyond the porch
Chronicling missiles and megatons, the joy
In his voice as he whispered, *Vaporized, vaporized,*
And more than him, the six-foot-six evangelist,
Last night of the revival, Bible wriggling high
On one blue palm as he rhapsodized on Armageddon.
I thought, *Christ eats the dead.* And think now
How the planet would turn as well without us,
As when a finger is lifted from a glass
And the water regains its shape, or sometimes,
Of a sudden, one night of childhood will clear
Above the general mist: a rock, a teardrop cedar—
We stand there linking hands before the fire,
Sing low, demand to hear the ghost story again,
Complain incessantly it is too mild unless
Blood drips from the banister and the headless
Woman shrieks and writhes up out of the fire.
We are not thrilled unless we are terrified.

3

Only in the tamed trembling of a poem, I had believed
Some kindness might survive, and "Cool your jets,"
He told me when I chided him for barging in late
And slamming down his books as I gravely read
Gray's "Elegy," a thing I shouldn't remember
Except it had a point. "Hey man, cool your jets!"
One of the teenage wisdoms: Beauty is final,
Devastating, absolute. In ugliness there is hope,
In trashed rivers, in the slightly obese girl
Who sat beside me twenty-five years ago as the bus
Groaned toward evil Tuscaloosa. And so I came
Like Amos to the black-light, pop-poster salons,
Read Vonnegut, heard the Dead, dropped mescaline
In numb, freaked-out America that year of Tet,
Said, "I won't go. I won't kiss the ass of death"—
But lacked the ossifying cool, the Stratocaster,
Ponytail, and rap that arched the backs of girls,
And so dug the French thing from Michaud to Villon
And languished in the rigor mortis of the *I Ching*.
And when Frog McEntire, God's aboriginal hippie, dressed me
For the drag ball—black midi and cultured pearls,
Matching bag, a platinum wig from the Dollar Store—
And squired me across the yard, a skeleton
Stooped and shat in a can. Four bikers roared
Up on hogs. He said, "Man, it's happening, and
I can't fucking believe it." He said, "Too much."
A bamboo screen, white kitchen, Jim-Ella's crowd
Raising blond dollops of hash on glowing spoons,
Gay, petulant, bouffant as Medusa's beauty shop—
And down the candled hall, black-jacketed Warhol,
Albino and amphetamined, beside his latest star.

## 4

This is the world sex saved us from: not fame
But indifference, not the moment of adulation
But the crowd dispersing through the alleys
Near the stadium, one season with its star
Dimming in empathetic roles, the nurse,
The guidance counselor, the sage of Mini-Pads,
Ascending the channels, eternities of Prague and Omaha.
In Carbondale, it comes in snowy, cracked, oblique.
"It's something in the water," a woman told me,
But the party soaked its last liqueurs. Jokes sobered.
A physicist spoke of a new calendar he'd devised,
Beginning after television, after the bomb. "We are,"
He said, "so terribly junior to that God."
When I was a boy, I loved my mother's biscuits
And feared the dark; deep space; vengeance
Of the desert prophets driving their vision dogs
Until the sexual animal was treed in fire.
"It's better," she said, pulling on lace panties
Behind the church, "when you believe in hell."
But it does no good to rub the times together,
Gabbling on that old string because we are strangers
In the peace that intervenes between lovemakings.
Or to see it all in an erupting instant given out
As when the artsies stroll all in black they know
It will fly apart, glass city, omnipotent, vulnerable.
And "God is orgasm," she whispered years ago
And lay back, small and white, on the dark rug.
It is not enough. It bores us and it works
As an ending only once unless we come to it without will,
And we come, stupid and crazy, believing in love,
And go winding back down the temple's easy stairs,

Near sleep, plummet past the owl and the mole,
And Twain wrote of ringworm as divine intervention.


5

After a while it occurs to us and at the simplest times
When the lights go suddenly out and we fumble
Lampward through the deep clutter of the rooms,
The past is mainly dark, but not what we thought,
Squirreled away in a box, all its books shut,
Its songs and anecdotes, previews of oblivion.
It will happen again, the terrifying sex, the light
Flesh makes blazing quietly underground,
Hendrix and Joplin, Morrison and Allman;
Talmadge, my childhood friend, Patrick's lover,
Who sang beautifully "How Great Thou Art"
And stewarded on the Chicago–London route
Before expiring, according to the local daily,
"From ambiguous complications of pneumonia";
Silly flowers on the ridge at Grayson Highlands,
Foxglove and wood sorrel, blueprints of mania
Where we sat and heard the charismatics testify:
*And when God called me to his service, I got*
*My hammer and saw, put the ladder in the truck,*
*And drove to Mexico. And built His holy church.*
Fog was lifting. Earlier rain had passed
East, whirled up the Holston watershed,
And now, as the light of the world came skipping
And dappling vague rosettes among the stones,
A man rose from the lee of the highest boulder
And spoke: *Brothers and sisters, strength*
*Is not enough. I ate steroids like candy,*

*Bulked up and benched five hundred pounds,*
*But it was emptiness until I accepted grace*
*And gave it up. The money, the cars, the girls.*
*And now, pump iron for Him, praise His name —*
*Listen, only a thin layer of skin*
*Keeps us from squirting into the world.*


### 6

This is the last testimony of the last days, made
On Sunday as cars rattle over the iron bridge
And on down Chautauqua, a stone and glass chapel
Founded on tax shelters, a modest Episcopalian miracle.
Light of the world, this is the joke love makes.
I was saved in Alabama and backslid to some good
Loving early in the colicky infancy of the bomb.
I hope my son won't run with zombies to the end.
The deal I'd rather make with the dead is fun,
The victories of peace: clean pillows, luxuries
Of orange juice and toast, which need no blessing,
Because the god sleeps, and nothing worships us.
No prophet rivets us to dread. No demon comes
On the tails of black jets, only iced tea and soup,
The Cowboys and the Bears, the endless human hope
That, backed up to the goal, insists that this
Is all there will be. This is all there will ever be;
But if you should read this, far off in the future,
Small and indefatigable dots, still holding on,
Still balancing on a blind tentacle of science,
Praise us that once we lay down without prevention
And started it, whatever it is salted in the genes,
Recessive trump that, of its own passiveness, waits

Through the unplayable hand and survives exactness.
Praise our uplifted thighs and the cries we made
As the seed harvest bared the singing nerve. Praise
Our electrons humming down cables from the split atom.
Praise the Beatles, W. C. Fields, and Bessie Smith.
Praise our many knowledges that came from accidents.
From our six fingers come your corrugating fins.
From our eyes come the balls of your reticulate feet.
From our brains your batteries. From our livers
Your encyclotropic perfumes. And if it is genesis
You would study, imagine us. We lived here.
We made our choice between the virus and the germ.

*Things That Happen Once* (1996)

# TV

All the preachers claimed it was Satan.
Now the first sets seem more venerable
Than Abraham or Williamsburg
Or the avant-garde. Back then nothing,

Not even the bomb, had ever looked so new.
It seemed almost heretical watching it
When we visited relatives in the city,
Secretly delighting, but saying later,

After church, probably it would not last,
It would destroy things: standards
And the sacredness of words in books.
It was well into the age of color,

Korea and Little Rock long past,
Before anyone got one. Suddenly some
Of them in the next valley had one.
You would know them by their lights

Burning late at night, and the recentness
And distance of events entering their talk,
But not one in our valley; for a long time
No one had one, so when the first one

Arrived in the van from the furniture store
And the men had set the box on the lawn,
At first we stood back from it, circling it
As they raised its antenna and staked in

The guy wires before taking it in the door,
And I seem to recall a kind of blue light
Flickering from inside and then a woman
Calling out that they had got it tuned in—

A little fuzzy, a ghost picture, but something
That would stay with us, the way we hurried
Down the dirt road, the stars, the silence,
Then everyone disappearing into the houses.

# MORTAL SORROWS

The tortures of lumbago consumed Aunt Madge,
And Leah Vest, once resigned from schoolmarming,
Could not be persuaded to leave the house.
Mrs. Mary Hogan, after birthing her fifth son,

Lay bedfast for the last fifty-two years of her life,
Reporting shooting pains that would begin
High in her back and shear downward to her feet,
As though, she said, she had been glazed in lightning;

Also men, broken on bridges and mills,
Shell-shocked veterans, religious alcoholics—
Leldon Kilpatrick, Johnson Suggs, Whitey Carlyle:
They came and sat there too, leafing through

Yellowing *Pageant*s and *Progressive Farmer*s;
One by one, all entered in and talked,
While the good doctor gargled a dark chaff
In his pipe and took down symptoms,

Annotating them on his hidden chart—
Numbness, neuralgia, the knotted lymph,
The clammy palms—and then he'd scratch
His temple's meaningful patch of white

And scrawl out his unfailing barbiturate prescription
To be filled by his pharmacist brother-in-law
Until half the county had gathered as in a lap,
The quantum ache, the mutiny in every house.

How much pain, how many diseases
Consigned to the mythological, the dropped
Ovaries, the torn-up nerves, what women
Said, what men wanted to believe? Part of it

Laughable, I know. Still I want someone
To see, now that they lie safe in graves
Beyond the vacant stores, that someone
Listened and, hearing the wrong at the heart,

Named it something that sounded real, whatever
They lived through and died of. I remember
Mrs. Lyle, who called it a thorn in the flesh,
And Mr. Appleton, who had no roof in his mouth.

# BEAUTIFUL CHILD

Because I looked out as I was looked upon
(Blue-eyed under the golden corm of ringlets
That my mother could not bring herself
To have the barber shear from my head),
I began to sense, as adults approached me,
That hunger a young woman must feel
When a lover seizes one breast too long
On the ideal nipple-balm of the tongue.
When they lifted me and launched me
Ceilingward, I seemed to hang there years,
A satellite in the orbit of their affections,
Spinning near the rainspot continents
And the light globe freckled with flies.
I could smell the week-old syrupy sweat
And the kerosene of many colognes.
I could see the veined eyes and the teeth
Dotted with shreds of lettuce and meat.
When I touched down, one of them
Would hold me to the torch of a beard
And goose my underarms until I screamed.
Another would rescue me, but leave
On my cheek the heart-mark of her kiss.
So I began, at three, to push them away.
There was no ceremony and few words,
But, like a woman who has let a man go too far
And, in one night's moodiness, steps
Out of a parked car and walks home alone,
I came suddenly to my life. They
Did not begrudge me, but turned back

To the things they had done before,
The squeaking bed, the voices late at night.
Mornings I'd crawl beneath the house,
Dreaming how poignantly tragic my death
Would seem, but, having thought about it,
I happily took myself into the darkness
Of the underground, where I was king.

# NELL

Not until my father had led her into the paddock
And driven her a month in circles and made
Her walk six weeks with the collar on her neck
And the bags of seeds on her back did he snap

The leather traces to the hames, for she was not
Green halter-broke when he took her that way,
Rearing and shying at each birdcall of shadow.
It would be another year in blinders before she

Began seeing how it would go from then on,
Moving not as herself alone but as one of a pair,
With the sorrel gelding of the same general
Conformation and breed shuffling beside her,

And between them only the split tongue
Of the wagon. As is often the case with couples,
He the subdued, philosophical one, and she
With the great spirit and the preternatural knack

Of opening gates, they had barely become
A team when the beasts began vanishing from
The fields, and the fields, one by one, fell
Before the contagion of houses. Still, they

Were there for a long time after the first
Tractors and the testing of rockets, so you
Could see how it had been that way for years
With them, just the one motion again and again

Until at dusk when the harnesses were lifted,
The odor that rose seemed history itself,
And they bent to their feed in the light
That would be that way for the rest of their lives.

# RISKS

I had not seen how dangerous the country was
Until he gunned it, downshifted into third,
And split the seam between the station wagon
Going east and the tractor-trailer going west,

The needle dead on the speedometer's horizon,
All of us tarred black from a day of laying pipe,
The cold Buds like tickets in our greasy fingers,
Him hollering fuckers and us begging stop

You son-of-a-bitch Jimmy stop this thing let me out—
We were going to college, we would be something,
And nothing like him, married, a dad at seventeen,
Though later, when we talked, it would be of him,

Stumbling home drunk at five A.M. to sucker-
Punch his father-in-law, then torch the garage,
As earlier, it had been of him, bolting from the cliff
Above the rock crusher, clowning through flips

For the first fifty feet, then knifing down clean,
The water so smooth, and him holding his breath
So long down there they said there was a cave
Under a big rock where he would come up,

Roll a leviathan joint, and smoke it as we stood
Arguing the details of calling the rescue squad,
And then he would surface with that same hard
Contagious laughter he had carried from childhood,

As he had always been the one holding it up to us,
The tattoos, the muscles, the slicked-back hair,
Sassing and taunting, even when he had gone
To Nam and the dozen shit jobs and the pen,

After the burglaries, the assaults, the homicide,
Him talking through our mouths, him clenching
Our fists, him never taking it from anyone.
And now—given the consecutive lives to think,

The nights in the cell, the days sewing wallets,
Pressing sheet metal into tags, loading laundry
Into chutes, hoeing the prison beans—does he
Think of us at all, is he even conscious of us

When he dreams he has us begging on our knees?
And when the blood starts, does he love us
Now that we speak of him often and always
With that sweet fear that marks our liberty?

# FIRST FRAUDULENT MUSE

Not seventeen, she dumped me.
No one has to tell me
A thing about the sorrows,
Aches, indiscretions,
And calamities of young poets
Of the United States
In the late twentieth century.
The poem I wrote then,
The one that would make her
Want me, either for my wry
Sensitivity or the scholarly erudition
Of my heart, is not this one.

It made some obscure reference
To the goddess Diana
While drizzling bad terza rima
About some poor decrepit wino
Eviscerating a garbage can.
My good friend looked at it
And made me know what
Kind of damn idiot I sure was.
His maxims come back—*read*
*Everything, love language, revise,*
*Abide in the transforming fire*—
And hers, mutated by distance.

While I was attaching the syllables
Of a certain mulberry tree
To an adjective that I loved,

She went and married an electrician.
Still I had to make a living,
Mindful of the preserving
Potential of the art,
And language clattering
Onto the platen like the small
Dark horse of the embalmer's salt.

Always it is the same night
I called her lily of the valley
And named her in many songs.
She keeps turning
Her cold beautiful shoulder
Into someone else's words.

# IN THE SPIRIT OF LIMUEL HARDIN

This morning some bald and wiry spirit,
Wreathed in smoke and shedding dark peals
Of laughter, has come down from the stand
Of cedars to hold forth to my father and me

Before retreating back into that soldery mist
Lifting above the portable sawmill.
Born the same year as my father, he is just old
And dying of emphysema, there is not enough

Breath left in him now to move the wing
Of a butterfly an inch from the scattering
Of chips cast by the blade of the saw,
But he laughs anyway, the laughter like

A fire that you draw up to, cupping your hands
And waiting for some ancient raconteur to squat
On his haunches and grub in the mulch
For a root to whittle into a box turtle

Before going on about the patient business
Of constructing oral history, but this morning
It is my father hemming and hawing
In that deliberate style that has marked

All his words since his stuttering childhood.
In his tale, everyone is dead or dying:
The Wilcutt girl, shot by her estranged husband
After he returned, out of his mind on dope,

And held the family hostage, the sheriff
Talking to him all night, convincing him
To let out the baby and the grandparents,
But then the silence, the scream, the shots;

This is supposed not to make us laugh,
But I laugh, and then Limuel gets started,
A dry chuckle at first, like a shaft turning
In the crankcase of a rusting Farmall,

And you can see it hurts, but my father
Cannot stop. Now it is the Pruett boy —
He had just moved here, he was working
Behind his mama's house with a bulldozer

Leveling the thicket for a trailer pad —
That boy had always been afraid of hornets.
Right up under that big walnut tree
Where the old outhouse used to stand,

Suddenly the hornets on him like a blaze,
He jumped, and a woman working nearby
Said that the track rolled over his head,
No one could find it, though she got there

So fast, his hand still gripped a cigarette,
A long ash, and the smoke curling up.
Sad, my father says, and nods,
But all the time, Limuel and I, grimly,

Secretly holding it, and now it comes,
The full-blown, gut-wrenching laughter,
The first hack, another and another, until
It has him on his knees in the wood chips,

Raising the inhaler, rubbing away the tears,
So we go over to him and help him to his feet
And walk with him as far as the spring,
And he goes on up into the trees, laughing.

# THE END OF COMMUNISM

Now I have Vallejo with me on the desk, his troubled words, and
    behind the words, his life tapped out
In Paris in 1938 while my grandparents shouldered one of the last
    springs of the Deep South Depression.
Vallejo, who felt compassion for the travails of oppressed laborers,
    would not have imagined my grandparents,
Dirt farmers and slaves of nothing but survival, with no boss but
    cramping hunger and penury,
The work of a few mild days wedged between the cold spells and
    the rains.

They waged their revolution against clods, and when they'd dropped
    their seeds, the main battles were still to come.
The war against the weeds yielded to the long August drought—
    stillbirths everywhere, cholera in the wells.
Maybe my grandparents would have had no compassion for the
    suffering of poets, who, even then,
Had time to dillydally over huge books and learn foreign languages
    and skedaddle halfway round the world and live
In impoverished splendor while they bent their youth against the
    cheating fields.

But when Bird Wilheit came starving and broke, they let him sleep
    in a room behind the house,
For which privilege he was given the field beside them to work, a
    place at their table
And the luxury of living fifty more years, a slave's son and maybe a
    slave himself. My grandparents loved Bird Wilheit.

I do not know that they would have loved Vallejo for writing what
    they already knew, that the world was a thief,
That many murderers sat far away in the feathery chairs of heated
    parlors.

They knew that someone somewhere knew more than they knew,
    and that such knowledge,
Imperfect and querulous as it must have been, was more than tall
    cotton and no salvation.
They knew work started in the bitter dark and ended in the bitter
    dark.
They knew prices were fixed against them, and to hell with it as long
    as everything
They watered and pampered into life did not die of floods or
    drought.

I have done a little work with my shoulders, back, legs, and arms. It
    has been a long time
Since I have done anything besides thinking, talking, and writing.
    What good is that
If it does not put a coat on someone's back? My grandfather, when he
    went into the nursing home,
Refused the government money. He was not rich, but neither was he
    broke. He worked.
Things came up. My grandmother moved beside him down the rows.

I do not know that anyone young will care what fomented the red
    dirt so I might fiddle with instruments
And read great books and mumble bad Spanish in my ripe Alabama
    drawl, but just because the shirt

On my back winds back to the drudgery of a field is no reason for
    guilt. I let the dead go on ahead of me:
My grandfather saying, "I reckon if you split up everything in equal
    parts, in five years the same folks would have it again";
And Vallejo reckoning "the enormous amount of money that it costs to
    be poor."

# A RIDE WITH THE COMMANDER

Suddenly, in the back of the boat, my Quinn of Mexico cap blown off
and shrinking

Behind me in the wake as we motor across the gulf, I look up to my
father-in-law

Hunched at the throttle the way he must have concentrated years ago
as he slanted from clouds

To dive-bomb a destroyer. I think, Just let it go, don't mention it, but then

He turns and, with his trained eye, gets a glimpse of it, bobbing back
there like a duck,

And then me, bareheaded: "Well goddam, why didn't you tell me you'd
lost it?"

By which I think he means not just the cap but how I've lived my life,
so undisciplined and regardless

Of money that why his daughter puts up with me he'll never know.
Maybe this is why

Now he jerks the boat so sharply that I'm slammed against the gunnel
before he gooses it with

Such precision that by the time he cuts the gas and idles alongside,
I'm sitting exactly where I was—

"Well, dip it out!" he says, and already as I snatch it, we're planing up
to the speed he loves,

The maze of mangrove canals behind us, the Pacific calm in the
distance, but choppy

In the bay's mouth, thundering as it masons its great white chimneys
above the shoals,

So just as we turn, I imagine the night sky lit with fire, and life risked
in terrible joy.

Another mile, we're gliding silently into the cove, and then, anchors
down, we're as we were:

Me sitting with the women, digging in the warm sand for clams, and
    him frisking
The icebox for a beer before wading out to stand in deeper water with
    men like himself,
Men with large voices, bankers raised in the Depression, merchants
    who have known war.
You can see this from the way they congregate equidistant from each
    other,
With their arms folded across their chests in equal poise—each has
    a secret
He would not divulge under any conditions, no matter the torture.

# ON PICKINESS

When the first mechanical picker had stripped the field,
It left such a copious white dross of disorderly wispiness
That my mother could not console herself to the waste
And insisted on having it picked over with human hands,

Though anyone could see there was not enough for ten sheets
And the hands had long since gone into the factories.
No matter how often my father pointed this out,
She worried it the way I've worried the extra words

In poems that I conceived with the approximate
Notion that each stanza should have the same number
Of lines and each line the same number of syllables—
And disregarded it, telling myself a ripple

Or botch on the surface, like the stutter of a speaker,
Is all I have to affirm the deep fluency below.
The Hebrews distrusted Greek poetry (which embodied
Harmony and symmetry, and, therefore, revision)

Not for aesthetic reasons, but because they believed
That to change the first words, which rose unsmelted
From the trance, amounted to sacrilege against God.
In countries where, because of the gross abundance

Of labor, it's unlawful to import harvesting machines,
I see the women in the fields and think of how,
When my mother used to pick, you could tell
Her row by the bare stalks and the scant poundage

That tumbled from her sack so pristinely white
And devoid of burrs, it seemed to have already
Passed through the spiked mandibles of the gin.
Dr. Williams said of Eliot that his poems were so

Cautiously wrought that they seemed to come
To us already digested in all four stomachs of the cow.
What my father loved about my mother was not
Just the beauty of her body and face, but the practice

Of her ideas and the intelligence of her hands
As they made the house that abides in us still
As worry and bother, but also the perfect freedom beyond—
As cleanliness is next to godliness but is not God.

# GROUND SENSE

Because I have known many women
Who are dead, I try to think of fields
As holy places. Whether we plow them

Or let them to weeds and sunlight,
Those are the best places for grief,
If only that they perform the peace

We come to, the feeling without fingers,
The hearing without ears, the seeing
Without eyes. Isn't heaven just this

Unbearable presence under leaves?
I had thought so. I had believed
At times in a meadow and at other

Times in a wood where we'd emerge
No longer ourselves, but reduced
To many small things that we could

Not presume to know, except as my
Friend's wife begins to disappear,
He feels no solvent in all the earth,

And me, far off, still amateur at grief.
Walking the creek behind the house,
I cross to the old homeplace, find

A scattering of chimney rocks, the
Seeds my grandmother watered, the
Human lifetime of middle-aged trees.

# SEX

It was when I read Lawrence that I first saw the world
As a prime lushness, an opening not to be refused.
Wonderful hairs, wonderful mysterious equations,
Each hedge dripping, each clock breathlessly ticking
In the heat of that transcendent, pollinating clarity.
Not a rock or tree that was not suffused with it.
Every bug-ratty spiderweb a doppelgänger
For the flimsy verbal chiffon that revealed it.
Each sermon, each lecture, a wire that carried it
To where I lay studying it, if I studied anything
More resonant than the tiles on the ceiling.
For even as I smudged real numbers on a grid
Or traced vectors to a nexus of force and speed,
My mind kept struggling manfully to represent
Its infinitely compelling budding and lubricity.
And one morning Professor Nielsen said with regard
To my heroic inability to accept what was given,
*Try to imagine a circle whose circumference*
*Is inside a proton, and whose center is everywhere.*
I have thought of it long as a figure for desire:
A patent for the ridiculous, one of the paradoxes
The need for grace conjures up from lassitude and greed
Like a logical boulder or a Latin-speaking frog.
Often it takes the form of a vulva or a nipple
When it is not moonlighting with the physicists
As a black hole in one of those baroque cosmologies
That lead us like a big head through blinding insights

Until we end up bodiless in a mathematical field.
But as the boy I was grows distant, he seems
Not me but some antiquated piece of fiction
Expurgated from the years and quoted by testosterone.
Beef and ambition, fluttering under damp sheets,
He hums his soulful ditty to the sixth dimension,
And for a while the god in his britches brings him
The ambiguous miscellanies and etceteras of pleasure
Like bisque that comes on a flounder-shaped platter
At La Lastra in Puebla, a deep and pungent gruel
Alive in black olives, the crab leg indistinguishable
From the eye of the octopus, and all of it compounded
In many spices, like those prayers of penitence
The young Baptists weep onto the altar cloth
Less because they are admissions of guilt
Than because they are truly elegies for promiscuity.
Wonderful hairs, wonderful mysterious equations
I could confess, too, now, as my early lusts
Begin ossifying into greed. I could counsel
Abstinence. I know the sorry old man is sorry
For something. One night a woman
Came to me, not as a tree or rock, but in the one fire
Of her true life. What has that got to do
With anything naked in the naked faces of children?
This afternoon I am barely aware of the young women
As they jog over the bridge into Thompson Woods,
But someone must stand very still in the shadows,
Listening to the gusts that come just behind them
As though the veil of matter had been ripped
All the way back to the light of the beginning.

I hear it, too, fainter and fainter. Then darkness comes.
Why should I praise the exemplary life,
Possible only in age or failing health?
All that I love was founded on the same premise
As heaven: that pleasure lasts longer than death.

## DIRTY BLUES

This young living legend leaning
Over the sink of the washroom
Of the Maple Leaf Tavern
Was not twenty minutes ago
Blowing the steel bolts out of
The twelve bars of "Stormy Monday."
Now I imagine he has
Come in from whatever
He kept briefly in the back seat
Of a buddy's parked car
To wash the fresh sediment
Of the flooding of the river Venus
From the skin of his prepuce.
Or is he just now anointing
Himself for some mystical
Communion to commence
Shortly in the scented
Cathedral of a stranger's mouth?
In a minute he will return
For the last set, the songs
So much alike, the women
Dancing with the women,
And the men lighting joints
In the courtyard where
The poet is buried. Just now
The way he goes at it
So carefully, from the tip
Back to the shaft, I think
He might be a stockbroker

Wiping a crust of salt
From the pores of a pair
Of expensive black wingtips
Before going in to purchase
Ten thousand shares
Of Microsoft. I know
It is none of my business
Where he comes or goes,
To what perilous conference
In the mean streets
Of the erogenous zones,
But I will tell my friends
Who wait at the oak bar,
Who will still be laughing
When again his music
Begins to darken inwardly.
This song he plays now
Is nothing but the blues.

# DON'T WORRY

Most of us are compositions that begin in error
And curl like telephones in the umbilical swamp
And break into the light, rending the living portal,
And after long waddling, stagger to our feet,
And after long goo-gahing, stutter into our voices.
Some would rather hear of Methuselah or Noah's ark.
A great many would prefer to meditate on springs
That slip right up from darkness unawares
And arrive, after much idyllic meandering, at the sea
Than imagine their fathers and mothers lost
To that act that often yields such indecorous mixtures
Of pain and pleasure we profane to call it love.

The talk that is only talk goes on talking its talk.
The priest talks to the pretty maid pregnant by a soldier.
She worries because there is war, or because soon
The war will be over, and there will not be
Enough work in the fields. The priest comforts her,
Saying this too will pass, saying what priests say
In the name of the Father and Son and Holy Spirit,
As if each child came with a loaf of bread under its arm.
The professional grandmother counsels her granddaughter:
Get on with it, get it over, just don't marry a fool.
When my cousin went on the pill, my aunt inscribed
Letters to Billy Graham and Norman Vincent Peale.

Young, and risking car sex without a condom
Because the least trespass of sheepskin or latex

Against the glans seemed sacrilege against Eros,
When I arrived at that stage where the seminal vesicles
Begin to secrete their first milky pearls
And the girl there with me had at last vanished
Into the riptide of her own unstoppable motions,
I would think of mangled bodies at accident scenes
Or old men in Bermuda shorts with tar on their legs
In order to hold back the spasm of nearly intolerable pleasure
That was just my own spring, musicking itself
From beyond volition, like a violin in a cavalry charge.

Passing the clinic with a friend, I see a woman
Bow out of a taxi and move through the chanting gauntlet
Of fanatics raising their pickled fetuses, photographs,
And bloody flags. When one with a greasy
Beard and a ring in his ear darts from the crowd
And spits the word *murderer* right in her face,
My friend shouts back at him from across the street,
Something stupid and forgettable, to defend her,
Who already has gone in to wait among the glossy
Plants and magazines, as though her own guilt
Had assumed palpable form and attached itself deep.
She sits there. It must feel almost as bad as being born.

What does a man know of *love?* His secret deliverance,
His blind spring joining the human river?
It flows darkly. It lasts as long as it lets him.
Because a man's immersion in pleasure stops
As it starts, he may spout bits of spasmodic wisdom
That seem leaked from the very plumbing of oblivion.
When my wife lay thrashing in the birthing room

Racked by the seventeenth hour of contractions,
And I passed a damp towel across her forehead,
I made the mistake of voicing the first words
That graced my mind, *I know just how you feel.*
She looked at me and said, *You don't know anything.*

## LURLEEN

We're talking Bosnia and eating veal but also lasagna
My wife's tailored for my friend's vegetarian daughters,
A collage of asparagus, mushrooms, onions, and cheese.

But cheese—there's the hang-up for one, who's so devout,
Her father explains, she won't wear leather shoes or silk.
Pure she seems, but also gregarious, taking her salad

Like a bridge, devouring her cabbage and peas as the talk
Unwinds a ticker tape of gang rapes, shellings, genocide.
When she's aware that I'm aware of her, she smiles.

No need to apologize, I know, but the way she watches
The veal transmogrify across the table, I'm wondering
If there's not, in the fine relish of her dining, an assertion

Of distaste. She doesn't say a thing. She sees
The juice coursing down my chin. I'm eating
Proust and Galileo, but she doesn't chastise. She's quiet

And unreproachful, laying into a leaf as if it were not just
Mushy fiber, but the vital, incarnadine tincture of a feast.
Also I'm wondering if it's consciousness that makes

Her good. Aren't women, by nature, herbivorous?
So I'd thought: herbivorous women, carnivorous men—
A suspicion I'd be hard put to admit, reared as it was

From such a tenuous complex of things, a botched
Sense of history, mother's cravings for beans?
Didn't Socrates warn against the philosophy

Of young men? They had, he owned, such a narrow
Phalanx of particulars from which to derive generalizations.
But what I felt at her age, those paralyzing sensitivities

To lives opposed to mine, the universe condensed
In each cell, and my indifference in the face of it all:
Wasn't that real, the longing for holiness, and terror,

When it seemed a normal walk across a sticky floor
To answer a phone might kill millions, maybe billions
Of microscopic lives, and one of them might be God?

Then there was the war, complicating judgment,
As now the wine begins to act on deeply plural whims.
Suddenly I want to blurt out everything I've killed

And eaten: rabbits, chickens, many fish, the sow
I'd named Lurleen for the governor's wife and raised
From a pig, things that seemed natural on the farm,

The killing and being killed, and knowing the names:
Important to know the things we eat, good or bad,
That is what I'd say to her of love. That or this:

"Lurleen," my father would say, "pass the Lurleen."
And I had an uncle who, as the cancer ate at him,
Began to love the cancer, even as he turned yellow,

Holding up the charts of his demise that showed
An alien thing going up like the wing of a cathedral
Before it took and whispered him up into the grass.

How innocently the desserts arrive, pale saucers,
Beautiful and sweet fruit, and the human afterlife
Wearing its grass to the ruminations of the cow.

Oh, my dear one, it watches us watching it.
We know, as it bends to the grass and lives,
The cow knows a few things that it's not telling.

FROM

*Elegy for the Southern Drawl*
(1999)

## DOWN TIME

Where there had been a landscape, I saw everything
Bare and no need for description, now that depression
Had soaked me up: no noise from the pine, the only green.
Sleep bore me on its inward-bearing gale,
Just blood veering off the bone, neither voice nor dream,
And when I woke, the weak music of sewage
Rushing behind walls. I needed to lean away
From the face no one would recognize, and the name
No one would call. If I could have imagined
That I was truly alive, I would have wanted to die.
Then, each morning, with a little less dread,
I went out and saw the frost on the lawn
And the awkward water frozen under the bridge;
But for weeks, in the birds limping on oily wings
Across the snow, and the foxes cringing
From dumpsters, I felt my life twinned
With everything that sinks, all the lost women
And men who, finding no door, sleep in the cold,
And the children, beaten down, foundering in disease.
How casually they seemed to bear the knowledge
Of their deaths. And then, poof! It was over.
Light took in the crystals of the thaw. I could
Look into the eyes of others without shame.
It would take time, and still, I was not there,
If there is here, excited again, on the other side.
Before the pleasure of lying with a woman,
There would be the pleasure of washing hands.

# DOING LAUNDRY

Here finally I have shriven myself and am saint,
Pouring the detergent just so, collating the whites
With the whites, and the coloreds with the coloreds,

Though I slip in a light green towel with the load
Of whites for Vivian Malone and Medgar Evers,
Though I leave a pale shift among the blue jeans

For criminals and the ones who took small chances.
O brides and grooms, it is not always perfect.
It is not always the folded, foursquare, neat soul

Of sheets pressed and scented for lovemaking,
But also this Friday, stooping in a dark corner
Of the bedroom, harvesting diasporas of socks,

Extracting like splinters the T-shirts from the shirts.
I do not do this with any anger, as the poor chef
May add to a banker's consommé the tail of a rat,

But with the joy of a salesman closing a sweet deal,
I tamp loosely around the shaft of the agitator
And mop the kitchen while it runs the cycles.

Because of my diligence, one woman has time
To teach geography, another to design a hospital.
The organ transplant arrives. The helicopter pilot

Steps down, dressed in an immaculate garment.
She waves to me and smiles as I hoist the great
Moist snake of fabric and heave it into the dryer.

I who popped rivets into the roof of a hangar,
Who herded copper tubes into the furnace,
Who sweated bales of alfalfa into the rafters

High in the barn loft of July, who dug the ditch
For the gas line under the Fourteenth Street overpass
And repaired the fence the new bull had ruined,

Will wash the dishes and scrub the counters
Before unclogging the drain and vacuuming.
When I tied steel on the bridge, I was not so holy

As now, taking the hot sheets from the dryer,
Thinking of the song I will make in praise of women,
But also of ordinary men, doing laundry.

# THE POETRY READING

And this is the way it had been done for years in the provinces,
With a nice young assistant decked out in tweed and denim
Standing up at the beginning to evoke some rusty quiddity
Or baroque valentine of the curriculum vitae
To tweak the vanity of the esteemed visitor,
Who would just then be wringing from a backpack
A handful of faded books and the new precious one
That had just from the soul been freshly delivered
And pressed in the black binder, from which
The torqued syllables would soon come springing.

This would be as a wonder to some:
Four who had already heard what was to be spoken
And loved or dismissed it; twelve who had dreamed
Of the ones they had heard of attending,
Who would take off their clothes for anyone;
Five who knew the name, but not the work
They had characterized often as promising or derivative;
And two who had blundered into the wrong room,
Thinking to learn of crocodile habitats
Or occult heresies of the Spanish Inquisition.

Still others would be here except that tomorrow
They would be called on to name the elements,
Trample a sonata, or defend a thesis;
If it did not happen on the night of the tournament,
Or on a day when debaters were flapping like puppets
From our greediest and most altruistic intentions;

Or at an hour when Christian bodybuilders
Had donned crucifixes and greased pectorals
To mount scaffolds at the center of the coliseum
And hunch in oddly hopeful positions.

But perhaps the university is not the place for poetry.
Picture our venerable line of shamans, bards,
And nervous wrecks, pulling themselves up
From the sticky kitchens of bohemia
To ascend the rungs of respectability.
Here one drones, whinges, signals with a fist.
Oh it is especially icky when the poet's
Less virile than his photograph, the African's
Too pale, the lesbian is insufficiently militant,
Or the lights make that noise of frying fish.

After all, not much happens in this lounge
Or small auditorium under the library,
And yet those who are here hear, don't they,
Among these lubricated delicacies for the auditory senses,
A thing that is right and singular to the heart?
Oh it does not always have to issue from guilt
Or some lingering inferiority to the British.
It can be done plainly or in elaborate meters.
Afterward, someone still unheard from
May actually go into a room alone and read it.

# REFUSING TO BAPTIZE A SON

Twilight came and my mother-in-law
Insisting again it would mean nothing,
The ceremony and the holy water,
And happiness of friends and family,
Which is everything to an old woman.
High tide at *el estero,* the Pacific roared

As beer turned to wine and wine to bourbon.
Midnight, fireworks, *Feliz Año Nuevo,*
And us, deep in our cups, and drinking on:
Me with my immutable gringo silence,
And her parrying, "What if he should die?"
And "You don't understand. You're not Roman."

What's changed now that she's buried?
Not nature, not my no, as dumb as yes,
Not the luck of the Spanish armada,
Or high muck I dreamed of defending:
Post-ethnic, post-religious, eclectic—
It's like her heaven. It doesn't exist.

Her spirit does. Stubborn. Procrustean. Loving
The palm tree's lovely freedom from knowledge.
May my son remember his grandmother
Alive in the tropics, standing for him,
Even in these words, even if they mark
The superstitions of an agnostic.

## NOT SEE AGAIN

Long I partied hearty with Hogdoo and weird Harold,
One of the hippies waiting the orbit of the strobing joint,
Talking sidemen on the liner notes of albums
And exotic booby traps of Cambodia and Vietnam,
Until, out of money, I compromised and took a job
Working beside Floyd, a pinkish African American
With tattoos up his neck and improbably orange hair.
Meeting, we'd hardly speak, passing the paper slip
We'd consult separately, filling the same order.

Loading boxes on the warehouse's high shelves,
I thought of the sports-car elect, free those afternoons
To motor past the magnolias and daffodils of Greek Row,
And assistant professors cooing toward whispering trysts
In borrowed efficiencies, and desperate women
Shimmying onto the mirrored stage of the Pussycat
To bare and jiggle their breasts for crystal meth.
But, also, oddly, each day I grew more attached
To the unspoken etiquettes of that work;

To the secretary Jane, who materialized each morning,
Split skirt flashing from her Triumph's green shine;
And to the men, each with his legend and games.
There was Dalton, infamous for his marriage
To an heiress; and Bayard, who'd served two years
For manslaughter after accidentally shooting
His wife while trying to kill another woman;
And others, remembered faintly from remarks:
"Boss don't fuck with me. He knows I'll cut him."

They called me Buttcut, Shorty, the Presbyterian,
And wanted to know what the notebook was for.
"I'm studying the poetry of Christopher Marlowe,"
I would say, and someone would answer, "Huh" —
Not that *huh* meant anything anyone would want to study.
Even shipping clerks know poetry means romance.
All day Floyd would croon at the top of his bad voice,
The Temptations, Otis Redding, or Stevie Wonder.
And one afternoon he cornered Roy, the foreman,

To say how the night before he'd met a woman
In a bar, and when the bar shut down, they'd gone
To a party way out in the country, a house, music,
Dancing, more drinking, and this is where it got fuzzy.
Either the lights had gone out and there'd been
A fight or there hadn't, but when he came to
The next morning, the car was missing and the girl.
Roy looked at Floyd the way a roofer looks
At sleet. "Goddam," he said, and shook his head.

But the next morning, daybreak, he picked us up,
And we rode around looking for Floyd's car.
Roy drove slowly, grunting as he sucked his pipe.
We circled, hollering to families on porches
Whenever Floyd seemed to remember a bridge or barn.
By eleven o'clock we'd stopped twice for beer.
It hurt Floyd to ask Roy for help, to admit
It wasn't the car, a rusted-out and bunged-up
Oldsmobile, he wanted to find, but the girl.

Roy spoke in an urgently deliberate patois
Of South Carolina, which seemed, in the way
The words got enjambed and the way the vowels
Dragged the voice through the consonants,
To be more singing impediment than speech.
Dalton mumbled of the fifties on the Riviera,
And, as he got drunker, Bayard kept pitching in,
"I told the bitch, come back, your ass is mine."
Okay, it wasn't poetry, but it made Floyd laugh.

We didn't find the car. Christopher Marlowe
Never finished his translation of *Hero and Leander*.
By dark we'd finished our last six-pack of malt liquor.
The stars had just come out. How lucky I was
To have gone broke, not to have it all regurgitated
For me from a book, but to have lain in a field
With the tongue-tied, the murderous, the illiterate,
And the alcoholic, since I've ended up like this,
The sedative raconteur, the contemplative man.

# PLEA FOR FORGIVENESS

The old man William Carlos Williams, who had been famous
    for kindness
And for bringing to our poetry a mannerless speaking,

In the aftermath of a stroke was possessed by guilt
And began to construct for his wife the chronicle

Of his peccadilloes, an unforgivable thing, a mistake
Like all pleas for forgiveness, but he persisted

Blindly, obstinately, each day, as though in the end
It would relieve her to know the particulars

Of affairs she must have guessed and tacitly permitted,
For she encouraged his Sunday drives across the river.

His poems suggest as much; anyone can see it.
The thread, the binding of the voice, is a single hair

Spliced from the different hairs of different lovers,
And it clings to his poems, blond and dark,

Tangled and straight, and runs on beyond the page.
I carry it with me, saying, "I have found it so."

It is a world of human blossoming, after all.
But the old woman, sitting there like rust—

For her there would be no more poems of stolen
Plums, of round and firm trunks of young trees,

Only the candor of the bedpan and fouled sheets,
When there could no longer have been any hope

That he would recover, when the thing she desired
Was not his health so much as his speechlessness.

# THE LIMOUSINE BRINGING
## ISAAC BASHEVIS SINGER TO CARBONDALE

A town is the size of a language.

In four more years he would be dead; but now,
A rare hot day in late April,
The middle of St. Louis
And the air conditioner didn't work,
The great black sedan
That Kenny had rented from Mr. D's
Quit, so they had to sit there for more than an hour
Before the tow truck and another car arrived,
Also black, two more hours to Carbondale:
The great man with the great drops
Of sweat registering on his brow.

Perhaps because the faculty
Of every backwater university
Endures by the prescient myth
That even to invite a venerable presence
To read in Starkville or Athens
Inevitably causes grave illness
And to have the person actually show up
Sets the leaves rattling above tombs,
Kenny asked, in that modest
And considerate way he has,
"Have you ever been in a car this long?"
"Oh yes, once in Sweden,
They kept me in a car for weeks."

He got here a little before dark.
He read slowly, deliberately,
A story called "The Missing Line."
When he had finished enunciating
Every word on a page, with a noise
Like a needle ripping the grooves
Of a warped 78, he would ratchet
The page from the staple
And lay it to the side and pause
To take an amplified sip of water

While everyone in the auditorium
Hushed to see if the great old man
Would push through the next hyphen—
Though, of course, the thing was,
The print was small. In the end
He would apologize, though all he did
Was to rush understandably from the elite
Of "The Missing Line" to the pica
Of "The Beard," omitting the last page
Of "The Missing Line." Though
All he did was to pretend to read
What now he began to improvise,
Mating the details of the two stories;
But then, suddenly, knew; was devastated, abashed;
And so had to backtrack and search
Awkwardly before three hundred people
For the missing closure, and so
Would write later, being an honorable
Man, and insist on returning the check.

He was a tiny man with big ears
And palms moist as opened pears.
At the session just after the reading,
When the professors of this and that
Were trotting out those tumors
Of erudition and septic ego
They like to pose as questions,
One of the more sensitive ones asked,
As everyone always asked,
"Why do you write in a dead language?"
And he answered without guile, "Luck."

The next morning one of the students
Asked him what advice he had for young writers.

"I wish someone would write about love."

He had the courage to be simple and precise,
And this would be the last of him.
He would not do it again, no matter the money.

A town is the size of a language.
It is not a language that you would have
Any reason to visit though it is not dead yet.

Nothing survives that has not been scarred
Lovingly in the brain
And dented by the human voice.

# SACRAMENT FOR MY PENIS

How do I approach it, bald as it is, dangling
Over the urinal to some golden expression
Of lemony bitterness, an old Trappist,
Blind in one eye, kneeling to his paternosters?
Is it mine? It never seemed to be mine.

It was old when I first saw it. A joke
Chaucer might have told but didn't.
A frumpish soldier slumped in a jeep
Above the caption *Dejected Nazi colonel*
*Waits to be transported to POW camp.*

Yet even now, in the spatulate dark,
Where it lies all day, secret as escape,
Sometimes it will leap of its own volition.
A young terrorist, sprung from prison
And bound for home, bent on sedition.

No, not that—here was my religion—look
Here, blue in the distances of skin—God
Flowers in this nerve. May it remain
Sovereign, inviolable, and unconfessed.
Honor most delicately this feverish guest.

# THE OBSOLESCENCE OF *THOU*

Last heard in a country church, in a prayer
That an elderly spinster had decked out
In what manner she thought befitting
For heaven's immoderate ears, it seemed
All a Sunday rite and benediction

Except some grave care in its blurting out
Made me think of the papa she'd tended
And kisses forgone for her all-mending,
Hands-on balm and alertness to afflictions
Just surrendered to the cemetery.

But also the way her prayer always ended
("Have thine own sweet way, sweet Lord,
Have thine own sweet way") broadened the context,
So I'd attach it to Pound wooing Keats
("Thine arms are as a young sapling under the bark"),

And love that did get made, often sweetly
(But how soon antiqued and caricatured) —
Not that I'd managed it yet myself,
Just that it seemed prudent to have some sins
To repent, and that one in particular.

# ELEGY FOR THE SOUTHERN DRAWL

### 1

It is all dying out now in a voice asking,
"Where you from? How ya'll folks doin'?"
On the blank verse of the forklift man,
From way off down there and yonder,
Is draining, thou and thine, from prayers
Of spinsters in the Nazarene church—
Is dying of knowledge of the world,
But still going, barely, in a grunted "hidey"
In the line at the cash register at Shoney's,
A father telling how he came north
To visit his son, impatience starting up
Its coughs behind him, his *yes'm*s and *no'm*s
An impediment here, Confederate money.
Kid's in my office, slow-talking. I ask,
"Where you from?" He doesn't seem to want
To say, thinks again, then does. "All over."

### 2

"Local area," my friend Beth Lordan tells me,
Was the code, in the hospital where she worked,
For genitalia, and she would use it
When she was bathing the old and infirm,
From the head down and then from the feet up,
Respecting that one spot, and one day,
Around the waist or the thighs, she stopped
Out of politeness, and asked an old man

Who was nearly deaf and dying of Hodgkin's disease,
"Do you want to wash your own local area?"
And getting no reply, asked again, louder this time,
"Would you prefer to do your own local area?"
At which he began to nod almost
Ecstatically, saying, "Dublin, Dublin."


### 3

The old people in the valley where I was born
Still held to the brogue, elisions, and coloratura
Of the Scotch-Irish, and brandished
Like guns the *iffen*s, *you'n*ses, and *nary*s
That linked by the labyrinthine hollers
Of the foothills of the Appalachian Mountains
The remnants of a people whose dominion
Obtained no less from unerring marksmanship
Than their spiteful resolve never to learn
Any tongue as remote as Greek or Latin,
Much less the Cherokee of Sequoya
That still haunted, like mist, the names of rivers.
"And there was May," my great-grandmother would say,
After May Collum's husband had been cut in half
At the sawmill, "lookin' like the hind wheels of destruction."


### 4

Country songs, sorghum, the odor of lard
That clung to coats, sweat and saliva roaring
Out of the varnish of old desks as the days
Heated up in late spring: it embarrassed me.
Until fourth grade, I spoke rarely, and then

With a hand cupped over my mouth, I began
To funnel sideways to my friends, as I write
Now in poems, the advantage of poems
In North America being that few will read
Who do not agree that the one in front of us all
Is dotard or tyrant, though at that time,
All the time I was learning the telling of time,
The names of county seats, and division,
I was blotching red with self-loathing,
And mumbling to mask the raw carcass
Of the mispronounced deep within myself,
Which was only the accent of the dying
Language of my South, which is a defeated country.


　　5

We're riding in the blue Oldsmobile.
Marvin's talking, telling the story

Of the tongue-tied butcher. He's
Working in the back of his shop,

Going with a cleaver at a side of beef
When another tongue-tied guy comes in:

"Cunh me a wump woast when you get tine."
"Fuh wih me you sumbith, I cunya head off."


　　6

*Do you know who this is?* the e-mail begins
As it has begun at least four times in the past

Three years, contemporary enigma, without
Accent or signature, only that once
We knew each other, though the language
Is too vague to suggest if we had been colleagues,
Neighbors, or lovers. *Do you know who this is?*
I know what it is to speak without knowing
How it will be received, to take a number,
To sway in a long-decadent tongue as on
A hammock stretched between two pining
Consonants, to audit the gross diphthong,
To pray *Do you know who this is?*, to sound
The vowels where the bodies are buried,
To be nourished by suspense, to emit
Unconsciously the still audioactive rhetoric
Of dead generals, to lie, to know yourself
The instrument and not the song, to wait
For the question *Do you know who this is?*
And not to answer, to become that very one—
*Anonymous,* everyone's favorite poet
Because there is no profit in it and no ego.


          7

When Big Jim Folsom ran for governor of Alabama
A gospel quartet rode in the bus with him, and before
He made the speech he always made,
They would stand on the platform and croon
The song he came to be known for, "Ya'll Come."

He promised to pave the roads, and he did,
And when he ran again, he said, "Before
My first term, I promised to pave the roads,

And I did. This time, I'm holding back one share
For keeping my word," and they elected him, and he did.

He drank, cussed, and philandered. Six foot seven,
Knowing himself, history. And the third time he ran,
A reporter in Birmingham said, "Govunah,
It ha' been repoated that last Sairday night
In Huntsville you slep wi' a nigra womah."

And Big Jim answered, "That's a damn lie,
Manufactured by unscrupulous demagogues
Who have little or no regard for decency,
Mudslingers who wouldn't square the truth
If it up slap and bit 'em. I didn't sleep a wink."


          8

I don't know what to say either. Eether/eyether.
"Don't make fun of me. I'm dead."

"You talk differnt. Where you from?"
John Brown asked Gloria—

Five years ago, cloudless Alabama day,
Us returning him to the trailer
From his job mowing the cemetery—

"El Salvador."

"Well, I ain't never been down
There in South Alabama."

9

Some kind of hippie cowboy on the elevator
Going up in the Music City Days Inn,
He's apologizing for his pink hardshell
Guitar case jammed in the closing door,
Thanks, and he's gone, the only white
Man I've heard speaking the hoarse,
Barreled-in English of a native of India.
Later, in the lobby, more cowboys,
Chaws in their mouths like extra molars,
Rhinestone collars, tight black jeans,
Luminous belt buckles, big fellows,
Talking Russian. This is Nashville,
Shrunken world, a hundred twenty miles
North of home. Anna Karenina,
Meet Minnie Pearl. At the bar
Of Tootsie's Orchid Lounge, where
All the rednecks used to dress like Johnny
Cash or Patsy Cline when they came
To be discovered, I stand a welcome toast
To the new line of wannabes: Yoruba
Dolly Partons, Cuban Robert Frosts.


10

Sometimes in one summer, one would hear,
In one family, four or five distinct accents:
Low-country mushmouth; mountain twang;

The almost *r*-less river-talk of merchant planters,
Droned out and of a lazy kinship to the sleek,
Ambidextrous blackspeak of their former slaves;

And the hated northun brogue, smuggled
Back from Dee-troit to parlay credit on a half
Pound of bologna and a box of Velveeta cheese.

Sometimes all of it perched there on one voice,
All the instruments in the symphony
Swaying on the skinny fife of a Scottish reel—

Though the old stuck to their *that there*s,
Their *this hair*s, *iffen*s, *you'ns*es, and *nary*s—
Murtis, this hair's my naiphew Graig—

A sentence that, except for the drawled-out
Eccentricities of the rhythms of that place
Between the Sand Mountain Plateau

And the Tennessee River, harbored
Only a hair shallower in the mouth than
The London cockney of a Lebanese immigrant.


11

When the Mongols conquered the Chinese
The males imitated them by wearing their pigtails
And adopting their every custom
Until, after centuries, the Mongols
Who were not married or settled
Lost their place, turned tail,
And fled back into the mountains,
Leaving the pigtail and certain words
That remain chiefly unremarked on,
And persist, like the classic poets

In the south of the North American continent
After two thousand years—just think
Of the ones who answer to Virgil and Homer.


12

In a recording of Faulkner's speech,
The words wallow and hover: *endyuah*
In a line all to itself, *prevaiah* like Isaiah

Salted and drying behind the tongue—
Just words—no human but the language
Grinding at the shackle of the quotation.

One way to learn a language might be
To forget yourself, ape everything you hear.
Another would be to shut up and listen.

When the line first stretched to our house
And my mother answered the telephone,
I could tell, from her emphasis of consonants

And the tincture and nasality of her vowels,
If she was talking to Grace or Modena,
A habit I hated in her the way I hated

In the exaggerated drawl of country singers
What I took for false emphasis, a pandering
To the cheap seats. Probably,

In retrospect, the way she carried on
With friends rooted closer to the mother tongue,
While the formal, slightly stiff constructions

And Latinate diction she typically used at home
Characterized the language of the country
Where she dreamed my sister and I would live,

Behind white fences, listening to Debussy
And reading Goethe and Shakespeare.
Though also she told the story of an uncle

Who, as a boy, mistook the meaning
Of *sophistication* for *constipation*,
A parable, perhaps, on the fantasy of diction.

She repeated it so often, it began to move
Like a rattletrap with kids hanging from
The windows, and many drivers.

"And how are you constipated ladies
Doin' this morning?" the punch line
Would go, and all of us would laugh.

*Particulars,* she would say to my sister
When she took a bath. "Don't forget
To bathe your particulars," because

The word *vagina* embarrassed her.
I feel odd hearing a tape of my own voice
That marks wherever I go, the sound

Of lynchings, the letters of misspellings
Crooked and jumbled to dupe the teacher,
Slow ink, slow fluid of my tribe, meaning

What words mean when they are given
From so many voices, I do not know myself
Who is speaking and who is listening.

# THE ASSAULT ON THE FIELDS

It was like snow, if snow could blend with air and hover,
    making, at first,
A rolling boil, mottling the pine thickets behind the fields,
    but then flattening
As it spread above the fenceposts and the whiteface cattle,
    an enormous, luminous tablet,

A shimmering, an efflorescence, through which my father
    rode on his tractor,
Masked like a Martian or a god to create the cloud where
    he kept vanishing;
Though, of course, it was not a cloud or snow, but poison,
    *dichlorodiphenyltrichloroethane,*

The word like a bramble of black locust on the tongue,
    and, after a while,
It would fill the entire valley, as, one night in spring,
    five years earlier,
A man from Joe Wheeler Electric had touched a switch
    and our houses filled with light.

Already some of the music from the radio went with me
    when the radio was off.
The bass, the kiss of the snare. Some of the thereness
    rubbing off on the hereness.
But home place still meant family. Misfortune was a well
    of yellowish sulfur water.

The Flowerses lived next door. Coyd drove a road grader
        for the county.
Martha baked, sewed, or cleaned, complaining beautifully
        of the dust
Covering her new Formica counters. Martha and Coyd,
        Coyd Jr., Linda, and Jenny.

How were they different from us? They owned a television,
Knew by heart each of the couples on Dick Clark's
        *American Bandstand.*
At dusk Junior, the terrible, would beat on a cracked
        and unfrettable Silvertone guitar

While he pitched from the top of his wayward voice
        one of a dozen songs
He'd written for petulant freshman girls. "Little Patti,"
        "Matilda,"
"Sweet Bonnie G." What did the white dust have to do with anything?

For Junior, that year, it was rock 'n' roll; if not rock 'n' roll,
        then abstract expressionism—
One painting comes back. Black frame. Black canvas—
        "I call it *Death,*" he would say,
Then stomp out onto the front lawn to shoot his .22 rifle
        straight into the sky above his head.

Surely if Joel Shapiro's installation of barbed wire and
        crumbled concrete blocks,
In a side room of the most coveted space in Manhattan,
        pays homage

To the most coveted space in Manhattan, then Junior
	Flowers's *Death*,
Hanging on a wall dingy with soot in North Alabama,
	is a comment, too.

Are they the same thing? I do not know that they are not
	the same thing.
And the white dust, so magical, so poisonous: how does it
	differ from snow?
As it thins gradually over many nights, we don't notice
	it; once the golden

Carp have rotted from the surfaces of ponds, there is no
	stench to it;
It is more of an absence of things barely apprehended,
	of flies, of moths;
Until one day the hawks who patrolled the air over the chicken coops
	are gone;

And when a woman, who was a girl then, finds a lump,
	what does it have to do
With the green fields and the white dust boiling
	and hovering?
When I think of the name Jenny Flowers, it is that
	whiteness I think of.

Some bits have fallen to clump against a sheet of tin roofing
The tornado left folded in the ditch, and she stoops there
	to gather
A handful of chalk to mark the grounds for hopscotch.

# THE SORROW PAGEANT

High and higher, beyond Guadalajara, the agave queuing up the sierra
    in diagonals strict as tombstones,
The road switchbacking to a narrow pass and threading to the next
    range, a line of trucks ahead
Grinding up into the invisible distance, the Bondoed wrecker in front
    of us, a wreck itself,
Gearing down with such gravity it seemed the whole load of bolts and
    rusty rebar
Would come right back on us, there then. As the gorge thing of
    postcard majesty and grandeur
Wallowed into clouds and reappeared in blowing pockets of clarity,
    we jerked to a stop-
And-go, stop-and-go, the minutes stretching out, with now and then a
    man in a cowboy hat leaping out
And stumbling quick to lift a hood and pour water into a boiling
    radiator, before the traffic palsied like a needle
In the hands of an arthritic seamstress. We came bump through a
    tunnel and there it was:
A tractor-trailer flipped on its side, and in the grass, blundering
    through the cloud of our bedazzlement,
What seemed at least two hundred hogs: some lamed and hobbling in
    circles; some kneeling
On broken gammons; and others, the gravely wounded, like pillows
    drying on the rocks;
The dead—no one had laughed yet, no one had said a thing, the gape
    like sunlight over everything—
"Because man is no longer a demigod," Joseph Wood Krutch wrote,
    "tragedy, in the classical sense, can no longer be said to exist."

O friends, do you know how the curtain in the brain comes down, and
    the part that will be played
By the public self primps for a moment: the phone on hold, the word
    unsaid? Don't peek there
Where the half-dressed ego counts its aesthetic money: two hundred
    hogs, two hundred Jews
On a train derailed on its way to a concentration camp, what the
    image must mutate to
If it's going to be serious, if it's a scene for the stage, if it's just
    conceptual art, an installation, a dance for radio—
The curtain goes up, two hundred cancan hogs who had gone riding
    piggy-piggy on their way
To becoming the chorizo of Puerto Vallarta. Why did I sit there
    stunned? Poor life, poor stumbling, doddering life!
Broken from its movable zoo and slaughterhouse bondage, so it was
    going to be animation, was it?
One Claymation pig, so luscious and pink, like Kathleen Turner in
    *Body Heat,* shimmied against our bumper,
And over there, blotto in the shade of a saguaro, W. C. Fields pigs,
    Oliver North pigs.
What had we seen before that the rules of looking depended on?
    Something from the beauty pageant,
Something for the newsroom that came in early on the wires and fell
    behind car bombings and assassinations,
And turned, by midafternoon, to a thing casually remarked on, while
    more glamorous sorrows,
Oil spills and hijackings, kept popping up until who would notice it?
    One of the duds,
One of the sweet odalisques from Omaha who did a campy tap dance
    but filled the swimsuit too full,
One of the Miss Congenialities of sorrow, perhaps to be lifted out
    on a day

When nothing much happened and no one was running for office,
and held against
The lady who lived to one hundred and eleven by eating nothing but
fish and never taking baths,
And the extinction of the pine shrew. I wanted the world to see those
two hundred hogs.
God rest their souls, I wanted to say. God bless their gouged hocks and
torn trotters. God bless the driver,
Dazed but still alive, standing off to the side with peasants who eyed
it all, feigning an air of companionable tragedy,
But wondering no doubt if the meat would keep and how to get it
home to adobe huts where,
Since they had their own TVs, they might learn how today a bus full
of nuns had tumbled
Down a ravine, or in some far-off and almost unheard-of country,
another monomaniacal pacifist was deposed.
I hoped they were the kind of men who saw the sweet humor, who
still believed in fate as perfect expression,
That before they ate, they would give thanks for the phenomenon, for
the miracle of those pigs.

## BLESSED ASSURANCE

Never, a brilliant woman told me, trust a man
Who has not been beaten. He will lack compassion.
I wondered, Could that be true? Exactly what
Did *beaten* mean? To look up at a brute
With his arm pinning your neck to the pavement
And plead to be let up, or to have taken
Crap year after year, until the countless small
Arrearages of spite had mounted sufficient gall
To sponsor a shit job that would rent a box
Between a fish market and a muffler shop?

While I chewed this mute host of questions
(what was meant by trust, and what, compassion?),
She drove and talked. I sat and listened,
Just old enough to conjure what had happened
With one man to make her think all men cads
By nature, only weakened to charitable acts
By a father's indifference or a mother's rage.
Did I think, too, of castration? In that age
The word *bitch* came pawing like a raccoon
At the garbage cans of young men's conversations.

And suspicions roared to mark the pratfalls
Of true love a man might suffer, if he lacked balls.
In all of manly silence there's a public caveat—
Not fists or threats, but what manhood's about:
Guard duty in our defeated warrior cult
Made me quiet and made the roadside clutter:

Wrecked cars in yards, chickens on porches,
Barns hardly distinguishable from churches
Where the minister's perpetually in trouble
For laying hands on a dimly languishing cousin.

I still defined *cynic,* all-seeing, half-listening,
Twenty years ago, as we rode to a poetry reading:
Our big day's mile-a-minute fields and rivers;
Between us, Diet Pepsi, octane of some wisdom
Of grandma's strained through Simone Weil—
But once I'd heard it clearly, another nail
In the coffin of things I'd secretly expected—
When Alabamians write the text on sexual
Harassment, the title will be *Good Breeding*—
Best concentrate on poems I'd be reading.

Soon we'd reach a city, its theater like a cyst
On the old train station. Did poetry exist
Down there in lingering dreams of horses,
In songs from the radio, and sacred verses
Children recite in vacation Bible school?
Or would our poems strike the vagrant local
Soul like spiced tea and the word *frisson,*
Funded by the Tri-States Arts Commission,
And followed by "I liked the one about the time . . . ,"
"I don't get it," and "Can't you make it rhyme?"

Down-home trust rhymes first with lust. Most
Live in private bewilderment, a kind of mist
Where stories keep bumping into questions:
That and religion's zodiac of generalizations
Comprise hick Zen and show how victims win.

But days don't end. They go on in the ruins
Of what's never trespassed, never spoken:
The good beating's southern as fried chicken.
Family or Christ may hide the chauvinist—
No southerner denies the bigotry of idealists.

*Kingdom of the Instant* (2002)

# A WHISPER FIGHT AT
## THE PECK FUNERAL HOME

### 1

No balm in heaven. Bone light. Things tick as they desiccate.

Immaterial who we were. Time narrows the hide to a strap—
Everything bound leaps once, and is free forever—
decay our fertilizer,
dissolution our daily bread.

Questions. Questions. Rain out there,
between here and the mountain.
Mist for the blind interpreter,
not here yet, maybe never.

But the body gets laid out by noon.
People like to have what is missing before them.

With ashes, you always worry, Are those the *right* ashes?

Corpse, I want to ask, silent mime,
are you packed?
The Ladies' Junior Auxiliary mans the train station.
What secret did you live out of like a suitcase?

## 2

Aunt Brenda took the spectacles out of a case
and placed them on the bridge of the nose.
Uncle Howard preferred
the unexpurgated face:

the valves of grief, just barely cocked, venting
a little into the overbearing politeness —

the formal versus the demotic,
the ancient grudge of the elder for the younger,
or Aristotle and Plato
transmuted to a whisper fight,

sounding something like
*kopasinkassubuk* and *hipatenudinsathat,*

until I thought to go out
into the hall and thank the undertaker.


## 3

The Summerfords were there, and the Minters,
friends of a life in the country,
church dinners, weddings, and harvests,
children growing up and going away.

What have I grown up to hate? Some
dishonesty in myself that in others
I could not face. A "scene." A scandal.
The private moment in the public space.

It used to disturb me, at funerals,
most of the people seemed so happy—
the grandnephews grand-funking in the parking lot
and the parlor, full of emcees and raconteurs;
even the widow chuckling
as she dabbed at one eye—

everything part of some vast,
mildly brawling syndicate of hypocrisy.


4

In high school, I would scrawl in the margins of textbooks
parodies of country songs:
"Always an Undertaker, Never a Corpse,"
"The First Word in Funeral Is Fun."
But death is serious. Condolence is the joke.

The undertaker gives permanents.
He takes the bald men's hats.

Once, when I was a pallbearer at the funeral
of a homicide, I watched
an old man, squint-eyed and sunken-gummed,
lean down and with one
nail-blackened finger probe the putty over the brow
where the bullet had gone in.

At least we don't hollow them out, wind them with rags,
soak them in tar, then execute their wives and dogs
so they will not have to enter paradise alone.

5

The wisdom stories are so bleak. No strawberries.

One asterisk, from a journal:

June 17, 1994,
the words
of Dr. Eugenia Poulos, she
was about to inject me with lidocaine:

*Don't worry,*
*I'm a good number.*

And another, later that week:

*The secondhand word of God*
*must have been a wise man wisely lying.*

*He has turned around since dying.*


6

What is the poetry of the world?
A wound and poultice.
An eavesdropper's serenade.
A shrug at Armageddon.
An obsolete love note
addressed to the vengeful cults
of longing and respectability.
Not music, not just music;

more like abandon.
The light of a conservatory
shining in the blueprint of a ruin.


7

Buddy Pittman, the undertaker, told me,
when he was fresh from mortuary school
and still alert to the possibility
of egregious error, he worked
the night shift, alone
among the steel tables,
and one night, nearly daybreak,
a body arrived.

If there was an accident and the doctors had to operate
but knew the patient would not survive,
when they shaved the head for surgery,
they would save the hair
in a manila envelope
to send later to the funeral home.

He told me this, smiling,
with the abiding confidentiality
of one who knows secrets
sometimes leak out into the open air
and get repeated, but he tells them
anyway, and they end up
on the Internet or in a poem,
for the world leaks.

And the corpse is always a local boy.
Had been celebrating high school
graduation, banana-strawberry daiquiris
fifty miles north,
and coming back, a head-on.
The familiar dry-county mortality.

They go out whole
and come back parts.
And you put them together the best way you can,
consulting as you work
the yearbook of the Tigers, or Devils, or Saints.

Fill in the gaps. Immaterial
what we were. The soul in heaven,
the body on earth. Labor
with putty and brush. Yeats's metaphor.
Makeup and art. All that work
for one performance and a matinee.

When Eunice came with the flowers—
the deceased was in her son's class—
she wanted a moment with the body alone.
Buddy must have waited like my students wait
as I read the poem of their life—
verdict, please, not critique. She was
a long time in there. Then said,
"You've done a wonderful job,
only Ronnie's hair was brown, not red."

8

The trick is always minimalism
and understatement, a sham

like civilization—
not the accurate representation

but one's own interpretation
modified by what one

imagines others expect,
a barely legible death

a paraphrase
of the face

most of the bereaved remember
him wearing into the home.


9

Before these words,
other words filled this page:
the aunt he never saw,
his mother's twin.

His mother. Dalliance,
encumbrance. A dot
of punctuation in the silent
history of maiden names.

His father married her,
pregnant with their second child,
on condition that she never speak
to her family again.

And that was Grandma Owen,
a vine, as I remember her in her dotage,
putting out the brown flower
of one hand.

Now I want something
that will stand for a man.


### 10

How strange our vision of another life,
even our own. The real life
storied to oblivion. The legend
nickeled-and-dimed by facts.

The cold eulogy works best, the painting with the fewest strokes,
the record, a verse or two, jokes
if the deceased was old, requiems for the young,
sometimes music, but never anecdotes.

He farmed and the farm got larger:
a natural Calvinist, in all things moderate,
work his middle name, husbandry his byword;
hated Wallace; admired more
than Kennedy or Lyndon Johnson
Adlai Stevenson,

that mild, unelectable man;
as an old man, loved girls, any girl,
modestly, with no trace of debauchery;

had been, in his younger days, a drinker,
a juror at the trial of the Scottsboro Boys.
What works always is silence. Never
imagine any truth desperate to be told.
Easy to love the world more than God.


11

They buried him with his spectacles off.
Closed the lid. Was.
I looked down at him. His or my bones.

I still eat at his table. For years I wore his shoes.

People like to have what is missing before them.

What temper he affected to hold.

He looked in death placid and composed as he had never been in life,
as if he had resumed thinking
the thought he was thinking before he was born.

# SMALL LOWER-MIDDLE-CLASS WHITE
## SOUTHERN MALE

Missing consonant, silent vowel in everyone,
pale cipher omitted from the misery census,
eclipsed by lynchings before you were born,
it cannot even be said now that you exist

except as a spittoon exists in an antique store
or a tedious example fogs a lucid speech.
Your words precede you like cumulus
above melodrama's favorite caricatures.

In novels, you're misfit and Hogganbeck;
in recent cinema, inbreeding bigotry
or evolving to mindless greed: a rancher
of rainforests, an alchemist of genocide.

You're dirt that dulls the guitar's twang,
blood-soaked Bible, and burning cross.
You cotton to the execution of retards,
revile the blues, and secretly assume

Lindbergh's underground America that sided
with the Germans in World War II.
Other types demand more probity;
you may be Bubbaed with impunity.

This makes some feel prematurely good.
They hear your voice and see Jim Crow.
But the brothers wait. Any brother knows
that there are no honorary negroes.

# A DEFENSE OF POETRY

If abstract identity, philosophy's silhouette, authorless, quoted,
and italicized, governs by committee the moments
of a mutinying, multitudinous self, then I'm lost.

But let a semi loaded with bridge girders come barreling
down on me, I'm in a nanosecond propelled
into the singular, fleet and unequivocal as a deer's thought.

As to the relevance of poetry in our time, I delay and listen
to the distances: John Fahey's "West Coast Blues," a truck
backing up, hammers, crows in their perennial discussion of moles.

My rage began at forty. The unstirred person, the third-person
void, the *you* of accusations and reprisals, visited me.
Many nights we sang together; you don't even exist.

In print, a little later is the closest we come to now: the turn
in the line ahead and behind; the voice, slower than the brain;
and the brain, slower than the black chanterelle.

The first time I left the South I thought I sighted
in an Indiana truckstop both Anne Sexton
and John Frederick Nims, but poetry makes a little dent like a dart.

It's the solo most hold inside the breath as indigestible truth.
For backup singers, there's the mumbling of the absolutes.
Du-bop of rain and kinking heat. La-la of oblivion.

Sheep-bleat and stone-shift and pack-choir.
There is a sense beyond words that runs through them:
animal evidence like fur in a fence, especially valuable now,

self-visited as we are, self-celebrated, self-ameliorated,
and self-sustained, with the very kit of our inner weathers,
with migraine, our pain du jour, our bread of suffering.

If poetry is no good to you, why pretend it can enlighten you?
Why trouble the things you have heard or seen written
when you can look at the madrone tree?

## BUFUS

We have founded a new kind of frog:
three-legged, one-eyed; or one-legged with three
eyes. Hops backward. Spongiform
tentacles creep its spine. Odd
to describe, like tubing around the heart,
an off *la* in the elemental rag.

Is Earth already whacked? How
address a prayer: "God Junior"? "Ms. God"?
The iron heats, the waffles pop.
But grace stings the meat. What a strange
duffel Brother Esophagus unpacks.
Taste quick. It's sewage down a pipe.

Void once meant filth. Frogs hopped
what grew from it. Now the jig's up.
Elimination spawns a myth.
Frogs lollygag under a rainbow
scrim of antifreeze and PCPs
or leap to prophets in songs.

Cinema sci-fi loves anthro-frogs,
orange planets of tight clothing
where cyber-sleuths glibly concoct
the quantum physics of a hop.
Ideal frogs are rainforest cancer cures.
The default frog's a caricature.

The default human's real, but how
weird to live in a body: looking out
but always staying in, not
knowing what's there and not,
and all the while beating against
the limits of perception like a moth.

I'm happiest, frog-like, in a tub,
ballooning a wash of ticklish bubbles.
Money swallows men and excretes cartoons.
Make everything simple. Water's
the central dodge. Everything
shed comes back as drinking water.

## FAMILY MATTRESS

It's in a permanent slump now, dry-docked
in the attic, an old, dream-battered raft,
striped as a convict, but how high it lay
mornings when I stole in to drift
down the resilient ether of its cloud

as though a schooner broke from the clods
of a field I had been hoeing, or I found,
among promises never delivered,
the risible helium of the soul
that woke in sudden divings and spinnings.

Here, too, my grandparents fell back swooning,
white-shouldered in the mercy of wings,
after conceiving my father and aunt.
To heft it now and wear it through the door
is to feel the weight of their weightlessness.

A coop smell rises. I am draped in myth
and the dried tallows and yeasts of tradition,
but set it on the floor. They will not mind,
who taught me music and setting hooks,
when I rip back the ticking to feather jigs.

# CHANNEL

*for Jon Tribble*

It had come up from the night depth of the lake to bend and chatter
    the rod as it lunged
under the boat, and now it flopped in the net until I had it in a
    slippery scrimmage on the aluminum floor:
suave as a satyr's haunch, but appaloosaed with dots, treble-spined,
    and whiskered like Confucius.
And now as I pliered open the jaws, and took the hook it had taken,
    it made something like a bee-buzz.
From deep in its mouth that was white as a ping-pong ball, it made
    something like absolution;
and then it curled in the icebox, whacking the beers with its tail;
    and still, there it was.
I do not like to hurt a thing alive, even a catfish, so slow to perish not
    even Saint Thomas Aquinas
or W. C. Fields could raise the eloquence to free its killer of guilt.
    In Florida, catfish walk.
Nailed to an oak, skin peeled like wallpaper, catfish won't stop talking
    with twitches.
But what they say improves on guilt. You have to have waited many
    nights, with your face
blackening from the smoke of burning tires, and shined your light on
    a belled rod ringing
over stones and going fast into the river, to know that their lives mean
    as much as your life.
And what is your life? The bottom of a shallow place? Magnificences?
    You hold them
carefully. You listen, and they say your name in ancient Catfish.

# HOMAGE TO MISSISSIPPI JOHN HURT

This morning when I went to play the scales
the strings of the guitar were so cold they might
have slept all night in the Holston's South Fork.
And the week after I bought it, while it traveled
between Herman Wallecki & Sons of Los Angeles
and southern Illinois, I dreamed
of a guitar so old it had weathered gray as a barn.
It had two necks, and when I touched
the bottom one to grab a C, the neck broke off
in my hands and wasps flew from the sound chamber.
But the tone of the strings on the other neck
was yours, old sweet-playing father.

In the late twenties, they cut a few minutes
of you into vinyl and sent you back to pick
and sing for nearly forty years in church and at parties
and to get by as a hired hand, practicing fatherhood.
Greatest of the fingerpickers, lost in dark mud,
two folkies found you in the singing vinyl
and asked, "How do you do that with a guitar?"
and searched maps of Mississippi for the town
Avalon from one of your songs, and could not find it
after all that time, so it seemed you were never there.

And what was there? Kudzu, polio, celestial darkness?
My band played Bumgilly, Nowhere, the cattle
auction, the armory in Wedowee, and our biggest gig:
the annual Fourth of July bash at the asylum.

But music has no place. "Mississippi has two cities,"
said Faulkner, "Memphis and New Orleans."
Upriver, the Vienna of the Delta is Clarksdale.
We looked for easy sevenths and found a covered
wagon drawn by eight mules, a beautiful dwarf
who leapt a rail to gulp down a crushed-out cigarette.

In the New York Public Library, on a nineteenth-century surveyor's
        plat,
the two folkies found Avalon,
drove to Mississippi, and asked at a general store,
"Have you heard of a musician named John Hurt?"
"Third road, turn right, house on your left, up on a hill."
So they found him on a porch and took him north
to become briefly, cogently famous and leave songs—
"Louis Collins," "Candy Man," "Make Me a Pallet on Your Floor,"
"Casey Jones," "Creole Belle"—
and return to Mississippi and die.

He was a little man, but cathedrals lit up in his hands.
When Segovia heard him, he asked, "Who is playing the other
        guitar?"
He darted and slurred, a syncopation, a waltz evolving to jig.
By slowing the record down and listening, a phrase
at a time, repeatedly, for six weeks, I learned
to scratch out a barely detectable rendition of "Funky Butt."
I do not like to sing, but sing, driving home from work,
sing to heal the language of its long service as a tool.

Greatest of the fingerpickers, lost in dark mud,
I do not know about the god of the fathers,

but to be born again in the tink and clong of a guitar
is better than to rot in a symphony of heavenly accountants
plucking the varicose vein of elderly harps. I know
a small man's largeness can be a pistol
in the dark, but it can also play. The name of joy is music.

# THE MASTERS

*from "Five Walks in the Nineteenth Century"*


When I began someone had already described
all the thoughts that might be suggested
by roots, what it is to go alone cold in twilight
down a country road past a cemetery,
all the ideas that were like leaves and boles,
all the dreams men had in factories,
and all the metaphors of mirrors and shadows.

Someone had used up all the women
with one arm and all the men with one eye,
and everything in the dump had been put
on paper and thrown into the dump
under other papers covered with the same words:
all the ways of smiling and drying one's hair;
all the unconscious, subliminal gestures

of pawnbrokers, short-order cooks, and stutterers
had been registered in the hallmark of sighs
and the museum of frowns; all the public
victories in private ruins had been ordained
in the scholarly journals and little magazines.
Both the plowed field and the barn
bursting with alfalfa had been set against

the works of Duke Ellington and Guglielmo
Marconi. No pixel of the ideal page
was not black with the traffic
of iambs, spondees, and double dactyls.
All the ways a tree might be said to speak
to a woman grieving the death of a child
had been claimed, purloined, reclaimed,

and readapted for pianos and violins.
All the words that had come into the language
in the last five years and all the styles
of exploiting one's knowledge of Latin.
Brake fluid, I thought, perhaps brake fluid,
but it was the age of tack and guy wires.

I would have to write a good pine tree
before I could walk the page recklessly,
missing the masters, but bolstered
by their absence, in it for the long haul
as if no poem had been made yet,
as if the poetry did not matter at all.

# MOSES

Moses is massive, as Michelangelo sculpted him for the tomb of Pope
    Julius II,
looking off to the side in outward vigilance while inwardly descending:
the face of a judge with the body of a mechanic or teamster; a fine
    delicacy of veins,
a muscular trauma in the stone, he seems to hide in revelation and
    exalt while suffering.

Clinton is six-three; Bush Senior was a little shorter, unless Clinton
    stood in platform shoes
while they debated. Dukakis lost to Senior, not because of Willie
    Horton but because
he was five-eight and, in the lethal advertisement, helmeted, waving
    giddily from the tank,
he resembled a peripatetic spud, as though the divine seamstress had
    run out of material
and attached the body of a presumptuous child to the brain of a
    grown man. A mistake. Though

only blemish suggests God to the cynic—a botch, a humanizing crack
    in the stone.
There must be terror. And Moses was tongue-tied. His brother spoke
    for him. So the law
opened, veiled in mystique, graven of a grave height and distance, and
    in this,
I am convinced, there is a secret wisdom, a fiction they must never
    know is fiction.

That Moses was himself Sinai: that is Michelangelo's secret.
    The image accomplishes
more. It bares the loneliness of a man who has seen God.


Mastery speaks for the design of politics, but politics is not art.
    Not usually.
Politics is like justice: blind, but less helpful, more forgiving. Art is
    mercilessly simple:
implicit everywhere one thing looks something like another, but
    more explicitly,
the thing itself, relieved by knowledgeable infusion, crafted, and
    distressed to beauty.
In Rome, you can see it now, in the basilica of San Pietro in Vincoli,
one of the few stones touched and improved by the human hand.

# TEN SIGHS FROM A SABBATICAL

### 1

Let loose. Lists into ashes. Tasks into stones.
In lethargy I revise myself. I loiter in the lily's canal.
Time to mood-walk among obsolete resolutions.
To drain rhetoric to all that does not speak and cannot listen.
Hello, thistle. What do horses hear?
A nap cleans me like a tooth. Mere duty rocks the hours.
The brain's self-whispering brushes the conscious event.
The face of a good friend is a breast.
A call comes in on the switchboard of the birds.
I swivel and skitter, a potato thrown through a warehouse.
I am injected with dream questions.
Instruct me, heavenly recipe for the worms.
How long must I be buried before I am done?
Rub me right, rule me, sweet other.
I'm old wood and new string.
I can only be an animal through this violin.

### 2

Who speaks now as if subject and predicate decree the world?
The trees were locked up, but have broken out.
I trail off down the sidewalk of an afterthought.
Only a busted cycle, Lord, a gleam spirited to rust.
What litters of darkness televisions own.
I'm a punched ticket swaddled by lint.
Come, eavesdroppers, hear the foreplay of obsessions.

A tsk-tsking, with a dumpty-do for variation.
Who else sits here, blues-measled, lonesome afternoons,
looking up follicle and Warren G. Harding
in *Compton's Illustrated Encyclopedia*?
Are you better than once, lightest foreshadowing?
Are you the largest amygdala in homeroom?


### 3

Pilgrim, what good there is for you to see
finds you. You don't have to look for it.
A lily trembles by a spring-fed brook.
Live children dream. A tax accountant
does a glum impression of Charlie Chan.
I'm off this year, dally to your dilly, yang
to your yin, but let me visit the office
once, friends open their mouths
to show the scars of humorectomies.
Why? Who's not wronged? Go cut a switch,
my own sweet mama used to say, and me,
I'd bring back a reed while my smarter
sister would present a gnarl of thorns.
But there's a glitch in utter victimhood.
The wronged-by-men-and-women face down
the wronged-by-God. Walk fast or run.
All verse writers moan, *Too late,* and zoom!
We're poster children for the irony telethon.

4

But oh to have come up with something new:
a minor amendment to a hairdo,
a twitch in a phrase, or chevron on shirt.
The will of others must be sidestepped after all.
If one is to reach into the pocket and bring up
like a magician's rabbit the gold eggs of the future,
one needs a tongue ring, earring, or mustache,
though in the case of bards, what dumb malaise
and spiritual laryngitis leave may be only
the aboard-saying panic and subliminal love sigh
of the greased consonants turning among vowels.
"Stretch out," they seem to say, "lay it all down
here in the seeds of the twenty-first century,
in the United States of America," and, "Baby, baby."


5

The great man, head like a cauliflower, addressed our poems
Thursday mornings, pontificating between coughing jags.
And what he said: "History includes you in this small way."
And what he meant: "Don't wake me up."
He who had sat with Cummings, Hart Crane, and Pound.

And what he remembered of all his time with Eliot:
"He never said anything stupid. He never made a mistake."

"Why are you doing this?" I asked, the one time we were alone.
"I'm giving my wife a horse or a swimming pool."

Cummings was a gentleman. Pound was genuinely batty
and believed himself Christ. Randall was jealous of Cal.
"Cal should be exonerated for what he's writing now."

He skewered Mallarmé: "A short poet with a long tail."
Then hacked at himself: "A quarrel with imitations."

He liked my poems best. Not much. I asked one other thing:
"After all these years, and books, what do you think of poetry?"

"I loathe and detest it."


6

The dead, when they are recent, are as good
as they will ever be. They do not bicker
or take the biggest share. They lie in state,
as well groomed and polite as ambassadors.
Done with the future, they hold to the past.
Soon enough it will be different, heavenly host,
God's moles, God's worms, God's nematodes,
Gabriels and Saint Peters of putrefaction: hello.
Blooms praise meat. But now an interlude. Now,
as never in elegies, the living prefer the living.


7

My father, for all my childhood, would oppose
my sighs as others might object to profanity.
If I had finished splitting a pile of logs
or loading a truck of hay into the barn,
I had only to lean back, inhale a great gulp

of air, and expel it with an undiminished *whew,*
and there he was like Marcus Aurelius.
Long I held tight, but now I give out
and go down the cleansing breath
dead-legged and bath-headed with joy.


### 8

Let loose. Lists into ashes. Tasks into stones.
Do the dead still dispatch scouts? Only
lunatics see angels. Surrealism's old-timey.
After fifty, the men in my family doze off,
even passionately making a point, intensity
of eyes coming down on you like a wake—
you start to answer, and we're off
in the slack-jawed, log-sawing sublime.
This clear gift descends on us like water.
Thunder brings out our highest power.


### 9

Release is better than ecstasy, downglide
peeled from the resistance of the living,
sockfoot in the meridian of twilight.
What picked the brain like a morel?
The honesty of things calls silently. Minutes
of committee meetings, doodlings
and scribblings make the soul's holy writ.
The rain says, Go and study with the birds.

## 10

It doesn't take much. Beautiful platitude:
All is delusion. In the right dark,
and if you are ignorant, brother,
a goose sounds like a coyote.
I'm looking for something a wren will approve.
One leak from the unlockable sea.
What's truer than fiction when it moves?
The peach in my own armflesh
makes me an agent of the sublime.

*New Poems* (2005)

# SALVATION BLUES

Many people here expect
the dead are not really dead.
Therefore, they resolve to live
as though they were not alive:

so softly the minor thirds,
so tenderly the major sevenths,
white gospel the elderly virgins
keep treading like chastity

until Franz Liszt, ravager
and destroyer of pianos,
critiques with a thunderstorm:

*Remind us there is something*
*to be dead about. Play like*
*you are alive, even if it is not true.*

# THE ATTITUDE

We who have towed the burden share a kinship
we ditch diggers and box toters
we hammerers and assemblers
no matter if we work now
as architects or engineers
if we enter a room primed with statistics
or quote Lévi-Strauss to a graduate seminar
we feel the boss lurking
in the aisles between the machines.
No, we will say, if you ask, Nothing is wrong.
Unless we are dying, the doctor is our enemy.

If we have ever crawled into a cold furnace with a hacksaw
or squeegeed into a manhole
or perched over a river tying steel
or gouged septic gums with spitsucker
or stripped the sheets from the birthing bed
or shackled the mad onto a gurney
or staggered from a fire ripping at a mask,
do not speak to us
of Tasmanian emeralds
or libraries in Korea.

We would prefer hearing what comes easy,
the Powerglide at the core of the transmission,
the profit that greases the laws into being.
Rich and beloved, we remain shitheads.
Before birth, we were cheated

by slag pits and rhetoric and mosquitoes.
Do not write of us. We will not read it.
Write the prescription that will make us gentle.
The trucks are empty. The boxes are full.
Show us what help means.

# ELVES

Where did elves come from?
a student asks, and John says,
*From Germany, I think they come*
*from Germany.* And childhood
fevers and tufts that thatch
the folds in an old man's ear.
On his ninety-fifth birthday
he began to remember what
he had never remembered:
a button on his mother's shoe,
the name of a neighbor's dog.

With faster eyes we might see them.
With medicine or sickness.
With malaria, I saw a wolf,
a wolf or a large cat: a cougar
or a leopard. I was never sure.
I go mindless in stairwells
and cloverleafs, the transport
out and the transport in. Now
I am withdrawing from nicotine,
a small elf, but gone in a fidget.

Gone the menagerie that chilled
and delivered me: the dog with
human eyes who explained
reincarnation; one silent dwarf;
and my personal beast, the troll.

Its favorite place was a bridge
near a school in North Alabama.
Elves prefer ancient elevators
that hang by a creaking cable
in a hotel of spiders and thieves.

They have tired of story circles,
of happy farms and children,
of being consulted and looked up
like footnotes or queries,
of vanishing deep in a book.
Elves only have to hear the word
*theme* and they begin to tremble.
In the ink that embalms
and makes them invisible,
their songs deaden to whispers.

*From Germany, I think they come
from Germany,* John said,
and the class resumed thinking
the thoughts that young people think
when not required to think.
Of beauty perhaps. Their own
and others'. And then jobs,
the bending work of the psyche,
all night and all day, forever,
hammers beating at the ore.

# THE BOOMERS TAKE THE FIELD

It takes a long time to forgive
heroism or beauty.
And then the young girl
in the old song owns a plot
in the memorial gardens,
a brow full of Botox,
and a lover with Viagra.

The laps of the mythical
parents of World War II
and the Great Depression
have lithified to granite,
yet we remain childish.
In our fifties, we study ourselves
studying their violence.

Do they forgive us our graduations?
They got dark early—
so elegant in photographs,
but thin from hunger
as often as vanity.
*We* were lucky, they said.
*We* should have lived in the thirties.

No one could find a kid.
Occasionally they'd find
a little person and beat it
for impersonating a kid.
And if it cried,
they'd beat it again, harder,
and give it a pair of Lucky Strikes.

# SOVEREIGN JOY

On the John Deere he felt inaugurated,
freshly minted, risen to eminence.
He could hit the left foot brake, square-
pirouette at the floodgate, and follow
the creekbank back to the barn. He knew
where liveth and when goeth and how
lift harrow and turn governor down.
He had studied paradise—this came close,
making a vow always to live right
and perfect corners he'd cheat by littles
until he went in an oval, round
and round, not seeing everything, but happy,
breaking ground, a farm boy with the Beatles
in his head, a young Baptist dancing.

# THE UNITED STATES

If you asked what it is all about
I would say a field a green field
in the turning rows a killdeer
and after that barbed wire
the hedge with its cardinals
a blacktop then another field

Corn one of the main things
after water and before milk
for whiskey is in it and grits
gold for chickens pearls before swine
there is a factory in every plant
if we could be properly humble

it is the greatness of the nation
along with cartoon animation
automobiles and rock 'n' roll
jazz and basketball evolved here
but not one other U.S. God
just the corn's imperial row

on row then Sylvester Stallone
and airbrushed Elvis thank you
very much ladies and gentlemen
Presley Dylan and the Supremes
no I would say a field a vast field
at the center top-hogs and cattle

then art the cities New York
Chicago Houston Seattle man
told me last week experts can
teach starlings to talk hell
televangelists may yet witness
in terza rima each stalk of corn

contributes it has been so
hybridized with its immense
ears it no longer resembles
maize it is what we have left
to barter for oil and microchips
tons of it siloed and elevated

to float us through droughts
and wars and speculations we ask
which most cogently represents us
*Leaves of Grass* or *The Simpsons*
there is the idea that every
living thing is a subset of human

control and the other notion
that though we may go on
a few hundred or thousand
years the poison has spilled
no more land will be made
the search for another arable

planet may prove moot as the
search for earthly sentience
meanwhile this taco here
crunches in the great scheme of
things we persist one people one
of the potential fates of corn

# MY MONASTERY

I saw a good deal of life.
Then I went into the university—
hallways, laboratories, books of the desire
to change government or art.

Very smart people, politically
committed, involved
with the latest theories, ambitious,
but as they aged, bitter, without purpose.

What had I thought on entering?
First, no more manual labor.
Second, all those nubile girls
at their maximum wildness and felicity.

Also the mean God of stupid people,
the divine thug, bigot, xenophobe,
executioner, and extortioner,
turned from the place in disgust.

I heard many opinions expressed.
The career pacifists, the Marxist
castrati could not stop singing
of the horrendous male ego.

Finally, universities honored
and sanctioned indigent forms
of noncommercial crafts,
the still-bearing crops of the obsolete arts.

It was a great life among the scholars.
Before that, I knew mainly
working persons—pipefitters, hairdressers.
I saw most of the United States.

Then books. Then interminable rooms
of people staring into bright boxes.
Before that a smaller light shone.
It came from short books into long silence.

Then Boccaccio crawled from Eve's apple.
Now if the golden vultures of Fox News
will stop flapping their two right wings,
I can watch the liberal arts die in peace.

What are words? Words teach the soul
to remember, and what is unknowable.
Many philosophies rubbed against my ear.
"You've been brainwashed," my aunt said.

She began that line when I learned the twist.
"Evil," she said, "sin." I think of her now
as my country lurches toward Baghdad,
big, dumb, smug, murderous, and born again.

# WINTON AND MILDRED

Harlan Baker and Charles Palmer had Winton Byrd
out in the drying asphalt of the new tennis court
pretending to be a statue, and now as he began
to struggle, they laughed and yelled "*Ree*-tard."
Is that clear enough for you? Should I repeat it?
In those days, they didn't socially promote you.
You stayed in grammar school until you learned
to spell Bull Connor or you died of arthritis.
If it matters, some of us learned that some
of the dead mattered, and the rest stayed where
shit belonged, inside quotation marks or italics.
The intelligent were tricky; the stupid natural
surrealists, good-natured provocateurs of laughter.
Once when Winton was a fifteen-year-old fifth grader
dressed in a leopard-skin suit to impersonate a caveman
in the spring operetta, he came by the back steps
of the junior high school where I was beating
a piece of angle iron against the concrete
and asked if he could try it. I let him then
and went on up to the seventh-grade classroom
where John Teague, professor of the facts of life,
comportment, and hygiene, told me to go on
outside, didn't I hear the bell, there was a fire alarm.
There was a fire alarm, and there came the truck,
And there came the principal, leading Winton
by his one spotted strap. Winton was a twin, almost
as good a thing to be as it was bad to be retarded.
If you were slow, the angels of orthodox sensitivity
who taught in the local public schools might,

after reading "The Tortoise and the Hare,"
assign you to the Turtles reading group,
but they would not separate twins. Did you ever
hear someone spell out something in front of you
so you would not know what they were saying?
When Winton's sister Mildred was fourteen and a fourth grader
she missed eighty-seven consecutive days of school,
and when she returned and the teacher asked what happened,
she answered, "I stubbed my toe." Mildred was not
a pretty young woman, but she was pretty enough.
I must be stupid too, because only today I figured out
what probably happened and who was involved.
I am not saying who. I am saying probably.

# AVUNCULAR

He told us lust would turn, transmogrify
to a plural version of mother love.
Friendship improved on that. A few
at sixty would give more
than they kept for themselves.

But parents, they had an expiration
date, like fish or milk.
They were like Jehovah with Jesus.
One day they looked up
and their duties were done.

How late he saw his orphan's portion of light.
And the spiritual life was surrogate.
Pacifiers and placebos. Only
perspective had meaning now.
Space-time, the anti-hubris, the hope

he might still marry,
if General Electric stayed up,
and become
some fifty-five-year-old's smiling
eighty-seven-year-old son-in-law.

# THE STATE-LINE STRIPPER

I got lost.
At a family picnic for the employees
of Martha White Self-Rising Flour.
Two lovers found me down by the Tennessee River,
a little fat girl
crying into the lichen on a stone's face,
and took me to the grandstand—

Embarrassing—
I got lost. And then I lost my fear.
Strangers and high places
and nightly publishing myself
naked except for a fireman's hat.
I danced and Jehovah's Witnesses
came unglued in the parking lot.

My creation was like the earth's.
In the beginning there was shame,
then the body after shame,
dangerous happiness—
If I could remember how I got here
I wouldn't be lost.

Yet my body recommends me.
All that I promised that I would not do, I did.
I got over my fear of darkness
when it seemed to me anything out there
would probably be better
than what shone here in the light.

# THE LOW-DOWN-SORRY RIGHT-WING BLUES

Not to be all things at once, but one sort or another,
a broker or systems analyst, may disappoint your mother,
but what luxuries accrue from playing a sure part:

shots of single-malt scotch and peg-hung copper pots
instead of doubts bubbling like newts in a cauldron.
A no-brainer keeps the beat. *Hard to feel bad. Hard to feel bad.*

Yet kitchen millionaires can't duck poverty's spirit
by fluffing superior crepes. Imagination is not experience.
The crop-duster drunkenly buzzing the country club,

the guidance counselor flashing her boobs in church:
these are inspirations, at least as much as popes
and principals. Even our Person of the Year,

the cardiothoracic surgeon who mans her own plane
and first violin in the orchestra, must sometimes itch
to botch a job. For ruin and the soul are involved.

Bums in their cardboard boxes are miserable. All right.
But only one can qualify as worst. The rest have failed
at being failures: alone with the gold in their mouths,

or gathered in caucuses of their commiserating
philosophy: Sorry. Sorry for what's done badly
or not done well, and sorry is what conservatives feel,

though they call it regrets and send it out in cards
that suggest the opposite. Christians who love
the blood-and-guts Leviticus-Yahweh more than Christ,

effective people, business leaders—still, they are sorry.
Welfare royalty light crack pipes with their tax dollars.
The best parties are always in the smallest houses.

# FEARS

They are like clouds on days
when there are no clouds, or flat
characters in works of fiction.

We go past them, knowing
that they stand near, breathing
but not fully vested, hovering

just shy of the third dimension,
traced lightly in pencil. That
they may have saved us once

from childhood embarrassment
or cauterized an ideal with a kiss
in no way qualifies them

for perennial attention. Go past.
Turn the page with a decided swish.
But as they live, I vouch for them:

the anonymous, the invisible—
these who have lost everything.
For them the bombs are not real.

They believe only in history.
They have no impression
that they leave an impression.

# COMMON-LAW KUNDALINI

A sudden loving settles into your own weight . . .
click, then roll over onto your back
and you are there above yourself,

the human spirit in full cloud-drift,
a lust fieldstripped to eye and ambition
which moves through walls and doors

and rises to the carnival of looking down
with no power but that of seeing
all of it momentarily unchangeable:

the shadow-tinseled moonlit fields
and silvery water towers on stilts,
the vole in the unblinking talon of the owl.

Even better, asleep, in dream-buoyancy,
I have seen more than I ever saw
pretzel-munching in some cloud valley

thirty thousand feet above the sorghum.
Once a pelican stopped to question me.
Once my friend Herbert McAbee

bumped into me out of the mist
with a talking sheep under his arm.
Often I have achieved much in basketball,

for many dream flights launched
from the magic floor of some actual gym
where old men smoked by a potbellied stove,

but removed from time, unblocked,
and watched by sweethearts, cheered,
I rose and dunked and hovered

with fear's iodine in my throat.
When I am up there, it is not poetry.
In the dream's onliness, it feels

wingless, bird-elegant, experimental,
requiring the decisionless decision-
making of dreams. But somehow,

why do I do this if not for the freedom?
Sometimes I wish I had never heard
of the name of Sigmund Freud.

## SITTING WITH OTHERS

The front seats filled last. Laggards, buffoons,
and kiss-ups falling in beside local politicos,
the about to be honored, and the hard of hearing.

No help from the middle, blenders and criminals.
And the back rows: restless, intelligent, unable to commit.
My place was always left-center, a little to the rear.

The shy sat with me, fearful of discovery.
Behind me the dead man's illegitimate children
and the bride's and groom's former lovers.

There, when lights were lowered, hands
plunged under skirts or deftly unzipped flies,
and, lights up again, rose and pattered in applause.

Ahead, the bored practiced impeccable signatures.
But was it a movie or a singing? I remember
the whole crowd uplifted, but not the event

or the word that brought us together as one—
One, I say now, when I had felt myself many,
speaking and listening: that was the contradiction.

# THANKSGIVING IN THE LATE FIFTIES

Hunting while the women cooked,
then coming in to the set table,
we took our sedative turkey
arguing politics and religion.

What waited after dessert:
dishes for them, and for us,
the Redskins and Cowboys.
The way women saw it

(while pregnancies condensed
in the kitchen and two-year
huffs spun from comments
on screen-wire permanents)

men were more predictable:
fourth-quarter cold warriors,
dozing together in the den,
fluttering like a string of bream.

# ON TORTURE

My people corrected children
as they had been corrected:
mildly—
          with switches and words,
never obscenities, more tones
of rebuke and disappointment.
Worse happened, welts
and salt baths, forced
wakefulness, electroshock—
genuine tortures, abuses.
We were aware of these.
Three houses down the road,
Charles, the homicidal
eight-year-old chain smoker,
mentioned a Louisville Slugger.
That might have been a joke—
the two faces of distance
like pleasure and his words for it.
Dirty words, what else?
Lord Therapy, arraigner
and creator of memories,
when did the truth ever
have anything to do with words?

# COURTSHIP

How much medication human mating requires
in the United States, in the twenty-first century,
gallons of beer and rum, kilos of hash and marijuana,
all to dispel the counsel of parents, and priests, and mirrors,
so every Bev and Bill can function as healthy adult creatures
and touch one cape of their erotic destiny.
And if the act succeeds, it replicates in more
and more fluent instances with ever less potent dosages.
And if it fails, the same drugs may aid in forgetting,
or multitask as anodyne and aphrodisiac
as ever so gently begin to billow the sails
of the ship of addiction on its ancient voyage to Mars
with the standard license issued by Venus.
Gallons of beer and rum, kilos of hash and marijuana—
Jesus is little help. He circles like a vulture.
Do you have baggage? the bellboy in hell asks,
and it is a suitcase Flannery O'Connor packed:
miscellaneous hair and skin and body parts—
the brain of one lover, the legs of another.
Funny, but very sad too, to love jealously
and know oneself unworthy of love, or not to love
and suffer for having to hurt a friend.
And crazy, isn't it, crazy love, when lovers drag each
other off like bones, and when they run to fat?
Dumped, they starve themselves beautiful again,
and, eventually, they talk, as all the tortured do,
"What kind of children would we have together?"
And they see them then: their future offspring in tiny
black robes, the justices of their supreme fun.

# THE LANGUAGE OF LOVE

It has taken thirty-five years to be this confident
of what happens between the noun and the verb.

Eventually, love goes. The image. Then the thought.
No? Then you are still alive. Only a little. And then,

I do not mean to depress you. Men have to hear
before they see. Sacred vows. Dropped shirts.

Women do not speak to men. They are overheard.
Sadness mounts people. Around the burn-scar high

on one thigh, the body of the beloved will vanish.
And the come cries and salt hair-smells of lovemaking.

Secret fiction, holy matrimony, longest short story,
the troth two lovers pledge to one another is none

of the president's business, let him say what he wants.
He is no good with words. Ask any true lesbian.

He should take a poetry workshop with Adrienne Rich.
He should try using the world less and words more.

# POSTMODERN CHRISTIANS

Men with holes in their heads,
children with gouged-out eyes,
rape victims, substantial people
with ripped-out tongues
in silent attempts at prayer.

Our mother who art in heaven,
why is there no gentleman
of sorrows of perpetual suffering?
Little boys need smaller fathers
than Mohammed, Moses,
Jesus Christ, and Joseph Stalin.

Little girls who blow themselves up
should never be referred to
as cowards or martyrs.
Men and women become ideas badly,
but the soul is a good idea,
even if it is not original or real.

The angels come to comfort us,
mother superior of agony,
because we know, every one of us,
only the unborn will judge us,
and they can't tell the difference
between a lifeboat and a leak.

# MY FATHER'S BIG IDEA

A stand of walnuts, by the board foot, would grow a fortune
in eighty years if one had the patience to wait
or knew descendants would hold the plantation.
But the land we inherit will be subdivided.
The farmer tenant who works it now can't afford it.
The man who will, who owns the rest home
and miles in every direction, has his bid sealed.
His mother, Alice, taught me in fourth grade.

He started as a bagger at a grocery, worked hard,
and bought the store, and then the home,
and now the county. For her I once crafted
a perfect to-the-scale replica of a log cabin.
Or more to the point, I boxed and turned it in.
It made, beside others, a frontier village,
a miniature Williamsburg, built by fathers.
Did she keep them? No one ever said to pick them up.

But thirty cabins a year for forty years?
Twelve hundred cabins, a metropolis larger
than our town, which disappeared, not
at once, but slowly, the way a walnut grows.
A thread goes back, the fiber optics of nostalgia.
But we are better off without land or farms.
No woman with one arm has to milk a cow.
No man has to follow a mule to a coronary.

My father says, One tree: six thousand dollars.
Eighty years, two hundred acres, twenty trees
an acre—I crunch the numbers Alice taught me.
At fifty, I see what my father saw. Walnuts
instead of shopping malls; trees, then furniture.
Dead, I am worth twenty-four million dollars.
But where does vision stop? Accounting?
How much is little? How poor does honesty go?

Alice Summerford, who furnished my mind,
liked to sit in the office of the rest home and read
Laura Ingalls Wilder during the last years of her life.
When I would visit, she remembered books I read
that seemed to connect things—money and family,
present and past, sons and fathers—a good
teacher, a great American perhaps, the first
to tell me I was adopted though I was not adopted.

# IN HIGH SCHOOL

We learn so much. And to what end? To make money
Being very good at something? To understand nature?
In nature, classroom equals captivity, spelling optional.
My class came out factory workers, truck drivers, teachers—
teaching, the one behavior teaching naturally teaches.
Teachers lionize Creativity, the common origin.
But study art and find the underground, the slums
of self-addiction, where self-expression matters.
Everyone else learns wolfing mush and following.
In gym class coed basketball, learn rebound, defend,
and pass. Forgo the shot. Those girls in the bleachers
have their periods but not too often. Gym teachers
hope delaying scrimmage will control boys the way
civics instructors plot to fend off natural history
with current events. Questions? Maybe two
more years of backward looks; then forget books.
Meanwhile, mark civics, p.e., and driver's ed instructors:
if these coach badly, they may evolve to principals
or guidance counselors. Nearly all the other faculty
spin languidly as the hand of a clock
from classroom to teachers' lounge to water fountain.
Follow directions, yes, but in poor schools, students
may call off classes or manufacture holidays.
As compensation, rich schools get swimming pools
and German classes. Leadership wins scholarships.
Take Latin if you can. In math and science,
deem chapters skipped essential. Some things

you can't forget. They are so right. Our principal's
name was Payne, a dapper man we remember
for his constant generosity, who retired suddenly,
moved to Birmingham, and opened a magic shop.

# VISION OF THE END OF THE WORLD
# IN THE VALDOSTA HOLIDAY INN

About the netherworld, I would rather live in Manhattan,
Kansas, and belong to the garden club,
except for Fiona Hubbard and Mrs. John Widman III,
who are setting up for a PowerPoint presentation
on November's topic: the care and nourishment
of cacti in the Great Plains. In the paper today
215 dead in Lagos at a beauty pageant riot,
and last night on C-Span, Salman Rushdie held forth
eloquently before I switched to another channel,
and lo, there appeared Louis Farrakhan saying
governments might have power, but his God
would bring earthquakes, tornadoes, and hurricanes.
When he said it, a fuse lit in his eyes, his voice shook,
and those big bodyguards drew in tight around him.
About the netherworld, some believe it is here now,
but Fiona Hubbard, in a cashmere cardigan
and tweed riding britches, is double-clicking on an image
of the desert rose, and Mrs. John Widman III
is saying one might be surprised how easily
it can be cultivated, even here in Manhattan,
where everyone who thinks she is not dead wants to retire
to Albuquerque or Santa Fe. Some cite
the days of sunshine, others miscellaneous allergies.
Salman Rushdie is a master. When it comes time
to answer, he has a way of turning
the spiteful questions around. Louis Farrakhan
reminds one of a wonderful little boy.
He can be hilarious with his understated apocalyptic

sexual innuendoes, and one can only admire
his capacity, in the length of one breath,
to segue from the laugh to righteous indignation.
As one watches first one, then the other,
one wishes that they could agree on a common text,
maybe the troops gathering in the desert
for the twenty-first century's first world war,
or perhaps it would be Fiona Hubbard's
and Mrs. John Widman III's PowerPoint presentation
on the care and nourishment of cacti in the Great Plains.

# OLYMPIAD

Between time and place
came this vivid consciousness
of things unalterable
that some, the lucky or
talented, might make
out of the materials at hand
in such a way that
they would last and be seen.

Others thought to work
not with mortar and stone
but with unspeakable cruelty
and human lives: it seemed
so obvious to these fate
might be impressed or
abetted only by slaughter.
No one need mention them —

they compete in all the books.
With their names we greet
and pacify the children.
The same games for centuries —
but they are not gods, not yet —
War artists, revolutionaries,
deathmongers, great men —
The first to become a god wins.

# RAIN ON TIN

If I ever get over the bodies of women, I am going to think of the rain,
of waiting under the eaves of an old house
at that moment
when it takes a form like fog.
It makes the mountain vanish.
Then the smell of rain, which is the smell of the earth a plow turns up,
only condensed and refined.
Almost fifty years since thunder rolled
and the nerves woke like secret agents under the skin.
Brazil is where I wanted to live.
The border is not far from here.
Lonely and grateful would be my way to end,
and something for the pain please,
a little purity to sand the rough edges,
a slow downpour from the Dark Ages,
a drizzle from the Pleistocene.
As I dream of the rain's long body,
I will eliminate from mind all the qualities that rain deletes
and then I will be primed to study rain's power,
the first drops lightly hallowing,
but now and again a great gallop of the horse of rain
or an explosion of orange-green light.
A simple radiance, it requires no discipline.
Before I knew women, I knew the lonely pleasures of rain.
The mist and then the clearing.
I will listen where the lightning thrills the rooster up a willow,
and my whole life flowing
until I have no choice, only the rain,
and I step into it.

# ACKNOWLEDGMENTS

Poems in this book first appeared or were reprinted in the following publications, sometimes in slightly different versions. *The American Poetry Review:* "Pastoral for Derrida," "At the Miracle Mall." *The Atlantic Monthly:* "For the Eating of Swine," "The Mosquito," "One of the Citizens," "Mule," "Beautiful Child," "On Pickiness," "TV," "Plea for Forgiveness," "Channel," "Sovereign Joy." *Blackbird:* "The Boomers Take the Field," "Common-Law Kundalini," "The State-Line Stripper." *The Black Warrior Review:* "Don't Worry," "The End of Communism," "Sentience," "A Ride with the Commander." *Crazyhorse:* "Dirty Blues." *Five Points:* "The Assault on the Fields," "Blessed Assurance," "Doing Laundry," "Sacrament for my Penis," "Ten Sighs from a Sabbatical," "Fears," "Rain on Tin." *The Georgia Review:* "Transparent Gestures" (originally published as "Caught"), "Every Day There Are New Memos," "Nell," "Moses," "Avuncular," "Winton and Mildred," "My Father's Big Idea," "The Low-Down-Sorry Right-Wing Blues." *Grand Street:* "Shame the Monsters." *Gulf Coast:* "Pussy," "The Kitchen Gods." *The Kenyon Review:* "A Blasphemy," "Elegy for the Southern Drawl," "Not See Again," "My Monastery," "Olympiad," "The Attitude." *The Michigan Quarterly Review:* "Contempt." *The Missouri Review:* "Winter Retreat: Homage to Martin Luther King, Jr." *New England Review:* "The First Birth," "I Find Joy in the Cemetery Trees," "Apocalyptic Narrative," "Grand Projection," "Thirty-one Flavors of Houses." *New Virginia Review:* "On the Bearing of Waitresses." *100 American Poets Against the War:* "My Monastery." *Poetry:* "For Those Who Miss the Important Parts," "Carpe Diem," "Life of Sundays," "Mortal Sorrows," "The Obsolescence of *Thou*," "The Poetry Reading," "Refusing to Baptize a Son." *The Poetry Miscellany:* "Sweep." *Poetry Northwest:* "Remembering Fire," "A History of Speech," "The Weepers," "First Fraudulent Muse." *Quarterly West:* "Sex." *River Styx:* "Elves," "High School," "Thanksgiving in the Late Fifties," "On Torture." *Shenandoah:* "Ground Sense," "A Whisper Fight in the Peck Funeral Home," "The United States," "Sitting with Others." *Solo:* "Postmodern Christians," "Salvation Blues." *The Southern Review:* "In the Spirit of Limuel Hardin," "The Sorrow Pageant." *Swallow's Tale:* "Decadence," "The Laundromat at the Bay Station." *Third Coast:* "Lower-Middle-Class White Southern Male." *The Virginia Quarterly Review:* "Thoreau," "Courtship," "The Language of Love," "Vision of the End of the World in the Valdosta Holiday Inn."

Reprints: *Alabama Poets:* "The First Birth," "Remembering Fire." *Are You Experienced? Baby Boom Poets at Midlife:* "Refusing to Baptize a Son." *The Best American Poetry* (1989, 1990, 1993, 1994, 2000, 2003): "Every Day There Are New Memos," "On the Bearing of Waitresses," "Grand Projection," "Contempt," "Plea for Forgiveness," "Ten Sighs for a Sabbatical." *Buck & Wing: Southern Poetry at 2000:* "The First Birth," "Ground Sense," "Remembering Fire." *First Light: Mother to Son Poems:* "Caught." *Handspun of Red Earth: An Anthology of American Farm Poems:* "The First Birth," "For the Eating of Swine." *Illinois Voices: An Anthology of Twentieth-Century Poetry:* "TV," "Mortal Sorrows," "A Blasphemy," "The End of Communism," "Nell." *Invited Guest: Twentieth-Century Southern Poetry:* "Remembering Fire," "One of the Citizens." *The Made Thing:* "Sweep," "The Mosquito," "The First Birth." *The Morrow Anthology of Younger Poets:* "Remembering Fire," "Thoreau," "The Mosquito," "The First Birth." *New American Poets of the '90s:* "Mule," "Caught," "The Weepers." *Poetry: A HarperCollins Pocket Anthology:* "Winter Retreat: Homage to Martin Luther King, Jr." *Poets of the New Century:* "Sacrament for My Penis." *The Pushcart Prize IX:* "A History of Speech." *Real Things:* An Anthology of Popular Culture in American Poetry: "TV," "On the Bearing of Waitresses." *Sixty Years of American Poetry:* "Nell." *Stand Up Poetry:* "Sweep." *Walk on the Wild Side: Urban American Poetry Since 1975:* "Romance of the Poor," "Progress Alley." *Western Wind:* "A Blasphemy." *What Will Suffice:* "The Bridge." *Writing Poems:* "Nihilist Time."